THE BEDFORD SERIES IN HISTORY AND CULTURE

The Congo Free State and the New Imperialism

A Brief History with Documents

- Justifications for the colonial state
- Native interpretations of
  Socio-economic & political transformat...
- Uniqueness of Leopold II's Free State

THE BEDFORD SERIES IN HISTORY AND CULTURE

The Congo Free State and the New Imperialism

A Brief History with Documents

Kevin Grant

Hamilton College

bedford/st.martin's
Macmillan Learning
Boston | New York

For Bedford/St. Martin's

Vice President, Editorial, Macmillan Learning Humanities: Edwin Hill
Publisher for History: Michael Rosenberg
Acquiring Editor for History: Laura Arcari
Director of Development for History: Jane Knetzger
Senior Developmental Editor: Kathryn Abbott
Editorial Assistant: Alexandra DeConti
Marketing Manager: Melissa Famiglietti
Production Editor: Lidia MacDonald-Carr
Production Coordinator: Carolyn Quimby
Director of Rights and Permissions: Hilary Newman
Permissions Assistant: Michael McCarty
Permissions Manager: Kalina Ingham
Cover Design: William Boardman
Cover Photo: Three head sentries of the ABIR with a prisoner, Congo Free State, ca. 1904.
   (front) Courtesy Anti-Slavery International; (back) Nancy L. Ford.
Project Management: Books By Design, Inc.
Composition: Achorn International, Inc.
Cartographer: Mapping Specialists, Ltd.
Printing and Binding: RR Donnelley and Sons

For information, write: Bedford/St. Martin's, 75 Arlington Street, Boston, MA 02116
   (617-399-4000)

ISBN 978-1-4576-5089-5

Acknowledgments

Acknowledgments and copyrights appear on the same page as the text and art selections they
cover; these acknowledgments and copyrights constitute an extension of the copyright page.

Foreword

The Bedford Series in History and Culture is designed so that readers can study the past as historians do.

The historian's first task is finding the evidence. Documents, letters, memoirs, interviews, pictures, movies, novels, or poems can provide facts and clues. Then the historian questions and compares the sources. There is more to do than in a courtroom, for hearsay evidence is welcome, and the historian is usually looking for answers beyond act and motive. Different views of an event may be as important as a single verdict. How a story is told may yield as much information as what it says.

Along the way the historian seeks help from other historians and perhaps from specialists in other disciplines. Finally, it is time to write, to decide on an interpretation and how to arrange the evidence for readers.

Each book in this series contains an important historical document or group of documents, each document a witness from the past and open to interpretation in different ways. The documents are combined with some element of historical narrative—an introduction or a biographical essay, for example—that provides students with an analysis of the primary source material and important background information about the world in which it was produced.

Each book in the series focuses on a specific topic within a specific historical period. Each provides a basis for lively thought and discussion about several aspects of the topic and the historian's role. Each is short enough (and inexpensive enough) to be a reasonable one-week assignment in a college course. Whether as classroom or personal reading, each book in the series provides firsthand experience of the challenge—and fun—of discovering, recreating, and interpreting the past.

Lynn Hunt
David W. Blight
Bonnie G. Smith

Preface

This book introduces students to the history of the Congolese peoples and the Congo Free State, ruled by King Leopold II of Belgium between 1885 and 1908. It illuminates historical debates over the infamous brutality of this regime as the centerpiece of Europe's "new imperialism" in Africa. After well over a century, the Congo Free State—often misidentified as the Belgian Congo, its name from 1908 to 1960—still resonates in both academic studies and the media. It has become legendary, its history a cautionary tale of how the avowed moral principles of European expansion were undermined and belied by greed. The humanitarian campaign against the state, driven by the Congo Reform Association in Great Britain, is treated as a point of origin for current methods of international protest by nongovernmental organizations, especially in the use of photography to validate allegations of human rights violations. The resonance of the Congo Free State owes much to Joseph Conrad, whose novella *Heart of Darkness* (1899) has become a touchstone of Western culture and remains a common subject of academic curricula and debate. Notably missing from most historical indictments of the Congo Free State and Conrad's novella are the perspectives of the Congolese peoples. This book challenges students to correlate and contrast different kinds of documents by Congolese, Belgians, Britons, and other Europeans in order to build their own arguments about life in Congo and the principles and practices of the new imperialism in Africa.

The reconstruction of events in the Congo Free State was a problematic process at the turn of the twentieth century, and it remains so today. This was and is the case because published testimonies by Congolese peoples were compiled and mediated by government officials and missionaries who were often skeptical of the veracity of their African informants and otherwise committed to their own goals of administrative control, profit, and Christian conversion. The details of particular, local events were regularly disputed, even as the now familiar narrative of the state's brutality became dominant in Europe and the United States. On the basis of a preponderance of evidence, the Congo Free State was and is roundly condemned, from Edmund Morel's scathing exposé *Red Rubber*, first published in 1906, to the many editions of Adam Hochschild's award-winning book *King Leopold's Ghost*, first published in 1998. Yet historians of Congo, like those of other regions under European imperial rule in Africa, confront difficulties in using a limited range of historical sources to move beyond general indictment and examine local experience. In the light of important scholarship by Jan Vansina, Robert Harms, and others, this collection offers students sources ranging from consular reports to oral histories, inviting them to establish an analytical method through which to discern both what people believed and what happened in Congo.

The Congo controversy displays the tension between the philanthropic declarations of European imperial regimes and the coercive practices on which the regimes' authority depended. At the outset of Europe's so-called scramble for Africa in the 1870s, the European powers generally subscribed to the paternalistic ideals of the "civilizing mission." This mission was famously described by the Scottish missionary Dr. David Livingstone in his call to enlighten Africa and abolish the slave trade through the extension of Christianity and commerce. This collection begins with Livingstone's vision for Africa as he described it in a speech at the University of Cambridge in 1857. There were those who believed that Europe's subsequent conquest of Africa—far from bringing light to the so-called dark continent—exposed Europe's own "heart of darkness" and a capacity for brutality far greater than that of any presumably "savage" society. In this regard, it is noteworthy that the Congo Free State's defense was based largely on its insistence that its policies and practices resembled those of every other European imperial regime in Africa, a charge now arguably sustained by leading scholars of colonial Africa. This book problematizes the common treatment of the Congo Free State as a uniquely terrible regime. A few documents portray the regime's methods not as exceptional but as typical of most imperial regimes in Africa at the time.

Contemporary debates over Congo included a new, radical critique of imperialism, which alleged that capitalists had effectively appropriated the imperial and foreign policies of European governments to serve their own ends at the expense of subjects and citizens abroad and at home. This book shows how this critique connected the Congo controversy to other contemporary imperial controversies by juxtaposing the writings of E. D. Morel, leader of the Congo Reform Association, and the journalist and social theorist John Hobson. Hobson's seminal book *Imperialism:*

A Study (1902) treated the Congo Free State as one example of the general effects of imperialism, which were also to be found in South Africa, China, and elsewhere. Echoes of this global critique can be heard today in debates over the motive forces behind military actions in the oil-rich Middle East and other resource-rich regions, including Congo.

Finally, the Congo controversy displays a variety of European visions of progress from savagery to civilization and divergent views on race and rights. Several documents demonstrate that Christian missionaries commonly rejected racial science and treated "heathen" customs and Islam as the main obstacles to bringing Africans to salvation. In other documents, critics of the Congo Free State simultaneously advocate the rights of the Congolese peoples and characterize these peoples as racially inferior beings. Meanwhile, officials of the Congo Free State and Belgian legislators in Brussels disavowed racism at the same time they defended their brutal regime. The sources in this collection challenge uniform definitions of racism and show instead how ideas of race and rights were historically contingent and interwoven.

Part One introduces students to the Congolese peoples, the environment in which they lived, and the process through which the Congo Free State was established and developed. The introduction acknowledges both the diversity of the Congolese peoples and the experiences and beliefs that many of these peoples shared. Turning to Europeans and the Congo Free State, the introduction examines the tension between the avowed moral principles of empire and the brutal practices of imperial expansion and rule.

The documents in Part Two invite students to explore these and other issues through speeches, international treaties, oral histories, investigative depositions on atrocities, visual texts, official and private correspondence, parliamentary debates, and published exposés. The documents are generally arranged in the chronological order of their content so that students can proceed from the foundation of the Congo Free State to the aftermath of the Belgian government's annexation of Congo in 1908.

Following the documents are a chronology, questions for consideration, and a selected bibliography of key secondary sources. Two maps showing the territory of the Congo Free State and the European partition of Africa, both in the introduction, help orient students in the region and the larger continent. The introduction, documents, and supporting materials will help students gain a better understanding of the Congo Free State and its impact on the Congolese peoples and on the processes through which the new imperialism took hold in Africa.

ACKNOWLEDGMENTS

Thanks to Lisa Trivedi, who is present in everything I write. Thanks also to Martine Guyot-Bender for lending her language expertise to this project. It was a pleasure to have the opportunity to work with a friend and discover that we collaborated so well. At Bedford/St. Martin's, I would like to thank Publisher Michael Rosenberg, Acquiring Editor Laura Arcari, Director of Development Jane Knetzger, Marketing Manager Melissa Famiglietti, Development Editor Kathryn Abbott, Editorial Assistant Alexandra DeConti, Production Editor Lidia MacDonald-Carr, Cover Designer William Boardman, and Production Coordinator Nancy Benjamin of Books By Design.

I am deeply appreciative of the comments and suggestions I received from the following scholars: Chris Agnew, University of Dayton; Antoinette Burton, University of Illinois; Tyler Fleming, University of Louisville; David Gordon, Bowdoin College; Candice Goucher, Washington State University; and Robert McLain, California State University, Fullerton. I should further note by way of acknowledgment that my creation of this collection has been guided largely by my experience in teaching courses on imperial history to students at Hamilton College since the 1990s. I was trained as a historian of European imperialism, not an area specialist in central Africa, so let me emphasize that scholarship by historians and anthropologists of central Africa has enriched my classes and my own research, which has focused especially on the relationships between imperialism and international humanitarianism. If this collection has succeeded in its primary purpose, students will find that it bridges the fields of African history, European imperialism, and international humanitarianism in its treatment of the Congo Free State.

Kevin Grant

A Note about the Translations

This collection of documents includes four oral histories by Congolese informants that have been translated from French into English by Martine Guyot-Bender, professor of French literature at Hamilton College. I selected these oral histories from among many others compiled by a Catholic missionary, Father Edmond Boelaert, in 1953–1954. Boelaert wished to record Congolese perspectives on the arrival of "whites" in Congo and the experience of common people living under the Congo Free State. The oral histories were published in the journal *Annales Aequatoria* in 1995 and 1996 and now constitute an extraordinary resource for historians.

The four oral histories in this volume (Documents 11–14) focus on the Equateur District of the Congo Free State and the territories of three concessionaire companies in which egregious violence occurred in the collection of wild rubber. This particular focus enables students to compare Congolese accounts with European accounts of the same area in the same period (Documents 15–17, 22). I cross-referenced the names, places, and events in these histories with other historical sources and works of historical scholarship to establish the time frame of each account. My footnotes identify, when possible, individuals and their professional positions. They also explain, again when possible, locations, unfamiliar terminology, and passing references. These footnotes may be of greater interest to the specialist than the general reader, but they suggest the depth and range of the many oral histories from which these four have been drawn.

Martine and I generally resisted the temptation to make grammatical corrections, choosing instead to maintain the grammatical inconsistencies and awkwardness that reflect the narratives' oral quality. For example, we have used the English present verb tense when the French text uses the present tense, even if the context suggests a past meaning, and we have kept the indefinite articles of the original text even when the context suggests that a definite article would be appropriate. Turning to the content of the oral histories, we have maintained the original place names and cited current spellings or new names in brackets and in the footnotes. Likewise, we have maintained the term "Arab(s)," which refers to Swahili-speaking Muslims from East Africa and Zanzibar. The reader will find that we have observed a distinction in the texts between a European's proper name (*nom*) and the nickname by which he was known among the Congolese (*s'appelaient*). With regard to narrative structure, we have left various loose ends untied and employed ellipses sparingly. In exceptional situations, we have inserted brief explanatory text in brackets. We have inserted or replaced text, as indicated in brackets, only in the rare cases in which we judged the text to be unintelligible to the general reader.

Contents

Maps and Illustrations

The Congo Free State and the New Imperialism

A Brief History with Documents

PART ONE

Introduction: Connecting Congo and the World

CONGO: PLACE AND PEOPLES

The Congo River brought change to Congolese peoples long before it carried its first European explorer, Henry Stanley, to the sea. The river transformed hunting grounds, relocated farmlands, and impelled villages to migrate across the floodplains of the central basin. The Moye fishermen distinguished seven seasons, each identified with a change in the river's flow over the course of a year.[1] These changes began at a distance, in the Rift Valley, from which the Congo flows to the west for approximately 2,900 miles in a crooked arc, first northward, then southward. Passing both below and above the equator, the river is watered throughout the year by steady rainfall and numerous tributaries that fuel its relentless power. Its entire drainage basin covers more than 1.5 million square miles; within the central basin alone, there are 7,500 miles of navigable waterways.[2] (See Map 1.)

By the nineteenth century, this riverain network facilitated extensive trade that linked most of Congo to a global system of commerce. Yet most of the Congolese peoples on the upper river had never seen a white man before Stanley arrived from the east, mapping the river from its source for the curiosity and prospective profit of Europeans and Americans. The British-born Stanley had been commissioned by two newspapers, the *New York Herald* and London's *Daily Telegraph*, to lead an expedition "to solve, if possible, the remaining problems of the geography of central Africa; and to investigate and report on the haunts of the slave traders."[3] The course

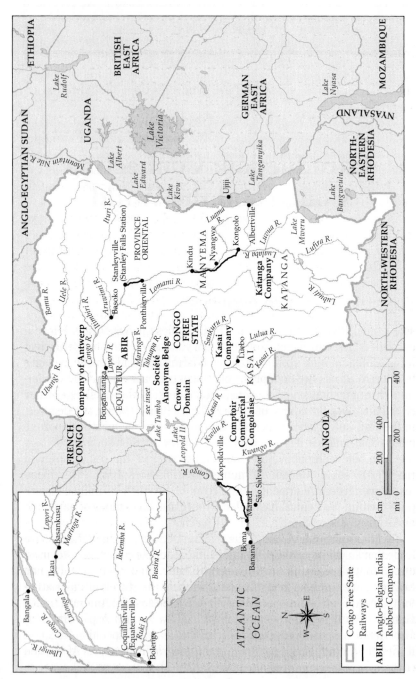

Map 1. *Territory of the Congo Free State, ca. 1906*

2

of the Congo River was the last and greatest of those problems. Stanley's journey ended at the mouth of the river on August 9, 1877, 999 days after it began. His accounts of the peoples and lands of the region captivated readers and sealed his reputation as the preeminent explorer of his era. His reports never reflected, however, on how the Congolese peoples perceived him. Rumors and stories of white men had long preceded Stanley to the upper river. They were conveyed by African traders traveling from the coast or the southern savanna, where these traders had exchanged goods with the Portuguese in Angola. On the basis of these travelers' tales, the Congolese peoples had surmised that whites came from a land beneath the sea—the spirits of ancestors returned from the dead.[4]

Geography largely determined the historical contacts between Congolese peoples and Europeans. The upper third of the Congo basin, located on the equator, holds the second-largest rain forest in the world, smaller only than the Amazonian rain forest of South America. To the south, the country is composed largely of grassy or wooded savanna. On the eastern edge, there are tropical highlands, and beyond them the Rift Valley. Surrounded by higher terrain, the central basin is a shallow depression, shaped like a fan, that narrows as it approaches the west coast. Flowing through the narrowing basin, the Congo River collides with the Crystal Mountains and backs up on itself at Malebo Pool before descending through 217 miles of cataracts. It settles again above Matadi, the farthest inland port accessible to oceangoing vessels, then rushes another 80 miles through the Congo estuary to the Atlantic Ocean, where it dissipates in a brown plume of sediment that can been seen for hundreds of miles offshore.

The Congolese peoples below the cataracts, on the so-called lower river, first met Europeans in the late fifteenth century, when Portuguese explorers encountered the Kongo kingdom. The cataracts blocked European travel to the upper river until the seventeenth century, when small numbers of missionaries and traders reached Malebo Pool on foot, traveling northward from Luanda along slave caravan routes.[5] The Congolese peoples living north, east, and southeast of the pool had little or no direct contact with Europeans until the later nineteenth century. For example, the Kuba kingdom, located on the Kasai River, a major affluent of the Congo River, was first visited in 1880 by a Portuguese trader named António Ferreira da Silva Porto, whom the peoples living there nicknamed Cingom, meaning "the gun."[6]

Congo was a dynamic and interconnected place that covered an area comparable in size to all of western Europe. A variety of social organizations, cultures, and economies existed there in the nineteenth century.

Forms of governance ranged from centralized kingdoms to egalitarian bands of people in the rain forests whom Europeans called "pygmies." Although there were linguistic differences between river peoples and inland peoples, the great majority of Congolese peoples spoke Bantu languages.[7] Particular ethnic groups, such as the Bobangi, monopolized spheres of influence along the rivers. Some chiefdoms, such as the Bushong, oversaw several ethnic groups with various languages.[8] Peoples of the rain forests traded wild game to farmers in exchange for food crops; they also hunted elephants and were often the original sources of ivory for the African traders who did business with Europeans. Many societies developed expertise in specific crafts. The Tio were well known for the production of raffia cloth, while other groups smelted iron or built canoes, the most expensive craft items made in the central basin.[9]

Most Congolese peoples shared important social structures and beliefs. Labor was divided by gender, and economies were generally organized at the village level. Slaves served many roles—from agricultural laborers to porters to wives. One could become a slave by being expelled or sold by one's kin group or by capture.[10] The selling and buying of slaves was more prevalent in the western basin and on the Congo River than in the east, until the eastern basin was invaded by traders in slaves and ivory backed by the sultan of Zanzibar and Indian investors in the 1860s.[11] Europeans commonly referred to the traders as "Arabs," but they were, in fact, Swahili-speaking East African Muslims.

Enslavement and any other adverse experiences were explained in terms of the "fortune-misfortune complex," an understanding recognized throughout Congo.[12] The most prominent features of daily life in Congo's religious landscape were interactions between the living and ancestral and nature spirits.[13] In the natural order of things, these interactions were good. However, there were also unnatural, evil forces that could ruin lives. Fortune depended on leading a good life and thus repulsing evil forces, while misfortune resulted from leading a bad life and bringing evil upon oneself and one's community. A good life was defined as benefiting one's community, while a bad life was defined as exhibiting selfishness. Within the fortune-misfortune complex, people attributed extraordinary hardship to witchcraft. If subjugated by Zanzibari slave traders or European forces, Congolese peoples were apt to look inward for some corrupting influence that had rendered them vulnerable to this evil. In times of crisis, communities sought and purged witches from their midst, believing that once they were free from the alleged witches, they would return to the good life. This is not to say that Congolese peoples did not recognize external responsibility for evil. Villagers sometimes nicknamed a European official of the Congo Free State *Ndoki*, or witch.[14]

Particular objects were believed to protect the individual and the community from evil, and such objects were central elements of all religious movements. Objects or rituals that served nefarious or otherwise selfish ends were deemed magical, not religious. These were the terms in which *ways in* Congolese peoples initially understood the symbols and rituals of Christian missionaries. In contrast to Christianity, religion in Congo was not doctrinal, yet Christian doctrine could be adapted to Congolese cultures because it seemed to explain important parts of the indigenous belief system, such as the creator spirit, which missionaries identified with the Christian God.

Throughout the nineteenth century, Congo was increasingly connected internally and globally by trade networks. These long-distance networks had originally developed in the eighteenth century to exploit the Atlantic slave trade. An ancillary effect of the slave trade in Congo was the expansion of trade in foodstuffs and crafts, which Congolese merchants loaded into any available space in the huge canoes that bore human cargo.[15] In this way, the slave trade integrated regional and global economies. While most of the profits went to traders, chiefs, and lineage heads, the less privileged also benefited.[16] For example, the main commodity traded in the central basin was the tuberous root cassava, a high-calorie staple of regional diets that was produced by small farmers.[17] With the demise of the slave trade in the mid-nineteenth century, the prices for slaves dropped dramatically, contributing to an increase in the internal slave trade of sub-Saharan Africa. Global trade nonetheless continued to connect Congo's regional economies as the exportation of slaves was replaced by the exportation of ivory, which Europeans used to make piano keys, billiard balls, and the decorative bric-a-brac of the parlors of the growing middle class.

Long-distance trade networks had not only economic but also cultural and social effects. Traders in the central basin developed their own currencies and language for doing business.[18] The trade between the interior and the coast introduced peoples on the upper river to European goods, such as printed textiles and various kinds of metalware, which eventually undermined indigenous craft industries such as cloth production and smelting.[19] It also facilitated the expansion of Christian missions, such as those of the White Fathers—Catholic missionaries who established their first stations along the trade routes for slaves and ivory between Zanzibar and the interior. Trade alliances between villages sometimes evolved into shared ethnic identities, and trade wars and piracy were regular threats to river traffic. Long-distance trade also provoked major incursions into and migrations within Congo. Zanzibari traders, who moved into the eastern basin in the 1860s in search of slaves and ivory, exercised control over much of the area until the early 1890s and provoked migrations of peoples westward.[20] This slave trade and the subsequent, coercive labor systems of the Congo Free State were arguably the most powerful forces that drove migrations in Congo throughout the late nineteenth and early twentieth centuries.

THE NEW IMPERIALISM AND THE FOUNDING OF THE CONGO FREE STATE

While still participating in the trade in slaves and ivory, Congo was transformed in the second half of the nineteenth century by another economic engine with global reach—Europe's "new imperialism." Historians describe this era of imperialism as "new" for a combination of reasons. Unlike the "old" era of empire building in the Americas, this period was not typified by mass colonial settlement, plantation economies based on slavery, or the acquisition and reexportation of commodities such as sugar and tobacco to other countries in Europe. Nor was it like earlier European periods of expansion into Asia, identified with trade in luxury goods, even though Asian goods such as tea had long reached the general European public. Instead, this new era was driven by Europeans' simultaneous search for raw materials used in manufacturing and for markets outside Europe in which to sell manufactured products. As Europe waited in the economic doldrums of the great depression between 1873 and 1896, there developed an informal alliance of industrialists, venture capitalists, and governments seeking not only economic but also strategic advantage over competitors in international commerce. They turned their sights to Asia, the Pacific, and, above all, Africa, where they soon made unprecedented advances with the help of new technologies.

Steamships and railways enabled Europeans to move quickly and in relatively large numbers beyond tropical Africa's coasts for the first time. Advances in weaponry gave them firepower out of proportion to their numbers. The breech-loading rifle became standard issue in European armies based in Africa after the 1880s; the Maxim machine gun was invented in 1884 and put to deadly use on the continent soon thereafter. Telegraph lines and underwater cables dramatically increased the speed of communication. The medical discovery of quinine as a treatment for malaria enabled more Europeans to survive and work in Africa, though diseases such as malaria and yellow fever remained prolific killers. Europeans were themselves vectors for other diseases, such as smallpox, that killed Africans in Congo and elsewhere.[21] European development in Africa entailed new labor migrations and faster transportation, both of which facilitated the spread of diseases already in existence, including sleeping sickness (trypanosomiasis), a parasitic disease that attacks the nervous system and is commonly fatal if not treated. As a result of the new imperialism, sleeping sickness became a transcontinental epidemic in the early twentieth century.

Although Europeans had been in Africa for centuries, this was the era in which they traversed the continent and established military dominance. In just the last quarter of the nineteenth century, more than thirty European regimes created a patchwork of sovereignties across Africa. (See Map 2.) Sovereign borders on a map did not, however, mark hegemonic power on the actual ground, as European governments consistently sought the greatest economic or strategic return for the least administrative cost. European rule in Africa was an expedient hodgepodge of administrations run by European governments or by private companies that European governments had sanctioned to operate in particular jurisdictions.

The new imperialism, made possible by steam engines, guns, and medicines, was characterized and justified by Europeans in moral terms as a "civilizing mission." This mission was defined by Europeans' belief that all peoples could be measured against a standard cultural or racial hierarchy of humankind ranging from savagery at the bottom to civilization at the top. Europeans commonly regarded Africans as benighted, savage peoples and claimed that they had a duty to raise these peoples to a presumably superior standard of civilization. This civilizing mission was strongly defined by Christianity and espoused mainly by missionaries, although European merchants and imperial officials readily invoked it as well. Dr. David Livingstone, the most famous European missionary and explorer in Africa at the beginning of the new imperialism, was widely identified with the civilizing mission in Europe and the United States. He was so famous that when he was feared lost in central Africa in 1870, the *New York Herald* employed Henry Stanley, then an unknown journalist, to go find him as a publicity stunt to boost newspaper sales. Although Livingstone was not lost, he was stranded in central Africa, where Stanley found him. Livingstone, for his part, found in Stanley an ardent admirer. When, after attending Livingstone's funeral in London in 1874, Stanley returned to Africa on an exploratory expedition that would conclude at the mouth of the Congo River, he believed he was continuing Livingstone's work.

Central to the civilizing mission was faith in the dual influence of Christianity and commerce, which Europeans believed to be a limitless

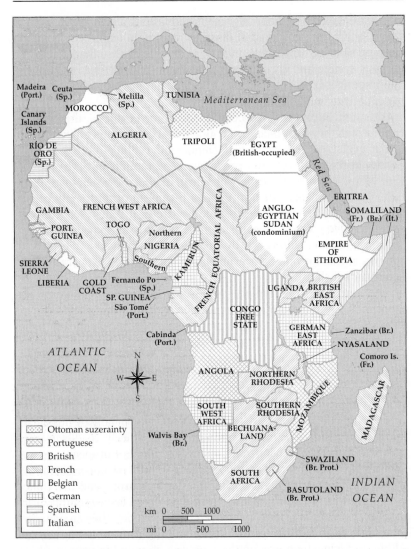

Map 2. *The European Partition of Africa, 1902*

source of moral and material improvement. Livingstone had famously declared in 1857, "Those two pioneers of civilization—Christianity and commerce—should ever be inseparable."[22] (See Document 1.) In the terms of the civilizing mission, commerce was a moral transaction and the decisive driver of civilization in three respects. First, so-called legitimate commerce would undermine illegitimate commerce in immoral commodities such as slaves. Second, it would facilitate Africans' assimilation of "civilization" through their adaptation of European material culture, such as European clothing. Finally, it would promote consumer desire, which would in turn inspire in Africans a presumably greater, virtuous work ethic so they could obtain more goods.[23]

After the 1870s, King Leopold II of Belgium, a monarch in search of an empire, became a famous, then an infamous champion of the civilizing mission. When Leopold ascended to the throne in 1865, Belgium had already begun to exploit its rich coal deposits to build one of the strongest industrial economies in Europe. It had a thriving textile industry, and it was expanding into steel, iron, and the manufacture of steam engines, rail carriages, and railroads. Unfortunately for Leopold, Belgium's leading industrialists had no interest in empire building. As a constitutional monarch, Leopold had significant political power, but he still needed to negotiate with a bicameral legislature, which was skeptical of his imperial visions. This skepticism stemmed in part from the fact that Belgium was a neutral state with only a small professional army, no navy, and no capacity to project military power overseas. Belgium's military was certainly no match for the militaries of its neighbors France and Germany, which had imperial interests and goals of their own.

Leopold believed that an empire would not only bring him riches but also increase his nation's prosperity and prestige, while concomitantly improving his imperial subjects through commerce. He was not particular about where his empire might be. He looked to Southeast Asia and South America before his attention was drawn to central Africa by the transcontinental journey of an Englishman, Lieutenant Verney Lovett Cameron, between 1873 and 1875. Cameron reported that the African interior held palm oil, sugar, minerals, rubber, and other commodities. Moreover, Cameron's description of the course of the Congo River suggested that beyond the cataracts Europeans might be able to navigate their way to the center of the continent. This potential highway into the heart of Africa entranced Leopold, who set his sights on Congo and began to prepare for his new role as an imperial monarch and businessman.

In September 1876, Leopold hosted the Brussels Geographical Conference, which founded the International African Association for the Exploration and Civilization of Central Africa, over which he presided. Invoking the civilizing mission, Leopold committed the association to combating the African slave trade and converting Africans to Christianity by establishing a series of stations along the same routes used by slave traders. He subsequently explained, "These routes and these stations, while serving as fulcrums for travellers, will powerfully contribute towards the evangelisation of the blacks, and towards the introduction among them of commerce and modern industry."[24] (See Document 2.) Leopold's resolve was strengthened by the news that Stanley had completed his journey down the Congo River in August 1877. Leopold hired Stanley, then in November 1878 founded the Committee for Studies of the Upper Congo, a nominally academic, essentially financial organization for Leopold's conquest of the region. In December 1879, this organization was renamed the International Association of the Congo (IAC), another ostensibly philanthropic front for the king's ambition. As Leopold's employee, Stanley traveled back up the Congo River that year and, over the next five years, used a combination of force, manipulation, and cajolery to get chiefs to sign treaties subjugating them to the sovereignty of the IAC. (See Document 3.)

Stanley established the bare framework of an imperial regime, including a road around the cataracts to what was then known to Europeans as Stanley Pool (Malebo Pool). (See Document 4.) Blasting his way forward with dynamite, Stanley acquired the nickname Bula Matari, meaning "Break rocks!"[25] Once the road was completed, he organized armies of porters to carry paddle-wheel steamers, in separate parts, up to the pool. There the steamers were assembled and launched, enabling Stanley to build stations for the IAC all the way to Stanley Falls (now Boyoma Falls) by the end of 1883. Porters carried forty-three steamers around the cataracts to the pool before the Matadi-Léopoldville railway opened in 1898, vastly increasing shipping between the coast and the interior. (Léopoldville, built on the banks of the pool, is now Kinshasa, capital of the Democratic Republic of the Congo.) The railroad itself took eight years to construct, at a cost of approximately two thousand lives, most of them African. Ninety percent of the capital invested in Congo between 1878 and 1898 went to steamers and this railroad.[26]

France and Portugal also vied for control of Congo at this time. Leopold outmaneuvered these two competitors by presenting himself to all the European powers as an honest broker committed to the benevolent expansion of Christianity and commerce. Harry Johnston, a leading British authority on African affairs, declared, "Nowhere, probably, does there exist a living philanthropist like Léopold II, who could from pure love of knowledge and civilisation open up a road across Africa for the benefit of the world."[27] In a series of bilateral agreements, most European governments and the United States recognized the authority of the IAC over Congo, making moral capital of Leopold's promises to support Catholic and Protestant missions and free trade, which together would presumably bring slavery to an end. European officials and merchants more discreetly welcomed the opportunity to exploit Congo without incurring the costs of governance.

Leopold capitalized on European rivalries driven by industrialization. Since the mid-nineteenth century, Great Britain's status as the predominant "workshop of the world" had been steadily undermined by industrialization in France, Germany, and the United States. In the mid-1870s, the British and French entered into stiff commercial and imperial competition in west Africa. This competition extended elsewhere on the continent until it was resolved by the Anglo-French entente of 1904. Meanwhile, Germany outpaced Britain in key industrial fields such as chemicals, then flexed its industrial muscles by expanding its military, which effectively pushed Britain and France into each other's arms. Recognizing growing tensions in Europe, the German chancellor, Otto von Bismarck, convened the Berlin Conference in 1884 to settle the general rules and boundaries of European expansion into west and central Africa. All the parties involved wished to ensure that a conflict in Africa would not trigger a war in Europe. Bismarck's particular geopolitical strategy was to exploit the rivalry between Britain and France in Africa to maintain a favorable balance of power in Europe, while blocking the extension of British influence in Africa for the benefit of German merchants.

Representatives of twelve European governments, the Ottoman Empire, and the United States attended the Berlin Conference and declared their goals in the moral terms of the civilizing mission. Their primary objectives were, in fact, security and trade, which they sought to achieve by investing the IAC with authority over Congo. They also pledged under Article VI of the Berlin Act, signed in February 1885, to watch over the Congolese peoples, "to care for the improvement of the conditions of their moral and material well-being, and to help in suppressing slavery, and especially the slave trade."[28] They additionally agreed to support the work of missionaries and scientists. (See Document 5.) Six months after the signing of the Berlin Act, Leopold unilaterally dissolved the IAC and declared his personal sovereignty over Congo as the head of the Congo Free State (l'État Indépendant du Congo).

In its first five years, the Congo Free State was a ramshackle operation that staggered under growing debt. Overseen by a secretary of state in Brussels, the government in Africa was led by a governor-general, four directors, and a military commander. The state's European agents—isolated at best, besieged at worst—participated in the existing trade networks that were still dominated by Zanzibar. Generally, these agents were no match for the Zanzibaris, as Walter Deane discovered in 1886 when a Zanzibari force compelled him to abandon and blow up his station at Stanley Falls. (See Document 6.) There was never a more telling sign of the early Congo Free State's limited power than when Stanley negotiated on behalf of Leopold to make Tippu Tip (Hamed bin Muhammed el Murjebi) governor of the Stanley Falls District in 1887. At this time, Tippu Tip was the most powerful slave trader between the eastern Congo and Zanzibar. This shrewd man had astutely calculated that the state was becoming a regional power that he would eventually be unable to defeat. (See Document 7.)

The Congo Free State depended on local chiefs who served it under the terms of the treaties negotiated or imposed by Stanley and other officials. Facing initial resistance from many chiefs, the state began in 1886 to organize a military, which after 1888 was called the *force publique* (public force). The force began with 2,000 men, 875 of whom were stationed at Boma and only 111 of whom were Congolese. In the first several years of the state's existence, the majority of its African soldiers and porters were drawn from Africa's west and east coasts.

DEADLY TAXATION

In 1887–1888, the Congo Free State's expenses exceeded its receipts by 10 to 1. The state avoided bankruptcy only because Leopold secured two loans from the Belgian government in 1888 and 1890.[29] The state then mastered its own fortunes over the next four years through diplomacy, taxation, warfare, and rubber. The main problems still before the state were its inadequate finances, derived from its primary trade in ivory, and the strength of the Zanzibaris. Its financial options were limited by the Berlin Act, which prohibited duties on trade. Once more, Leopold exploited the discourse of the civilizing mission, this time in cooperation with the leading Catholic abolitionist, Cardinal Charles Lavigerie, the archbishop of Algiers and Carthage, who saw in opposing the Zanzibari Muslim slave traders a chance to check the spread of Islam in Africa. (See Document 8.) Leopold might have failed to mention his employment of the Muslim slave trader Tippu Tip when he agreed to work with Lavigerie to convene the Brussels Conference in 1889–1890.

At this conference, which was devoted to ending the slave trade and liquor and arms trafficking in Africa, Leopold persuaded the European powers to permit him to create a new system of taxation in Congo for the purpose of combating the slave trade and building a stronger infrastructure for governance. In the two years after the conference, the Congo Free State instituted a new tax system in which African chiefs were forced to collect and pay taxes in goods and labor.

Furthermore, in 1891, Leopold arrogated all "vacant lands" in Congo, as well as the present and future produce of those lands. "Vacant lands" were defined as any lands without a human settlement or crops under cultivation. Leopold thus placed the greatest part of Congo at his disposal, putting an end to free trade in most of the state's territory and enabling him to gain revenue by circumventing the Berlin Act's prohibition against trade duties.

Leopold then enjoyed a stroke of luck. The mass manufacture of pneumatic tires for bicycles by John Dunlop in Dublin, Ireland, after 1889 generated a dramatic increase in the demand for rubber. Companies subsequently produced not only tires for bicycles and, later, automobiles, but also rubber industrial components, such as hoses, and consumer goods, such as toys. Europeans had already discovered wild rubber in abundance in Congo. Rubber quickly replaced ivory as the Congo Free State's main export to Europe in 1896.[30] In the midst of the rubber boom, Leopold gave tens of thousands of acres of land to three concessionaire companies—the Anglo-Belgian India Rubber and Exploration Company (ABIR), the Company of Antwerp for Trade in Congo (Société Anversoise du Commerce au Congo), and the Anonymous Belgian Company for Trade in Upper-Congo (Société Anonyme Belge pour le Commerce du Haut-Congo, or SAB), all founded in 1892 for the purpose of extracting rubber and ivory from the rain forests in the region of the Lopori and Maringa rivers. Leopold held major investments in these companies, so he stood to profit even as he relieved himself of the costs of administration.

To enforce its new tax system and prepare for a decisive confrontation with the Zanzibaris in the east, the Congo Free State began in 1891 to augment the *force publique* with forced levies among the Congolese. The *force publique* grew from 1,487 in 1889 to 19,028 in 1898.[31] Between 1892 and 1894, on the strength of more stable finances and this growing army, the Congo Free State conducted a successful war against the slave traders in its eastern territory. It was further strengthened by the combination of a final loan of 7 million francs from the Belgian government in 1895, a lucrative trade in rubber, and its ruthless system of resource extraction.[32] Between 1890 and 1901, the revenue from Leopold's lands in Congo rose from around 150,000 francs to more than 18 million francs.[33]

Captain Guy Burrows, a former commissioner of the Aruwimi District of the Congo Free State, estimated that by the mid-1890s there were only 670 Europeans in the upper Congo, about half of whom were state agents. "These white officials," Burrows observed, "are stationed in some fifty Government posts, each . . . the administrative centre, so to speak, of 14,000 square miles more or less. To properly administer such a country under existing conditions is clearly a physical impossibility."[34] Relative to the massive size of the state's territory, the number of state employees did not grow dramatically in the years ahead. There were 684 in 1897, then 1,031 in 1900.[35] Burrows, an Englishman, personified the cosmopolitan composition of the state's personnel and the white population in general in Congo. Of some 3,000 whites in the Congo Free State in 1908, about half worked for the state, 20 percent were missionaries, and 30 percent were private merchants. Roughly 1,700 of the total were Belgians, most of them members of the Belgian military employed by the state.[36] The other 1,300 were drawn from all over Europe and North America.

There were some consistent characteristics of the Congo Free State between the mid-1890s and its end in 1908, when Leopold ceded power to Belgium's elected government. The majority of state employees were concentrated on the lower river throughout this period, and even after the mid-1890s there was no disciplined, effective administration above Malebo Pool.[37] There was, however, a system of taxes to be paid in produce or labor for the benefit of the state, concessionaire companies, and missions. These taxes were obtained locally through people appointed as chiefs by the regime. The collection of taxes was generally overseen by one of several concessionaire companies, the agents of which exercised autonomous, discretionary authority in their interactions with these chiefs and their villages. The agents' demands and decisions were enforced by African sentries posted locally and, if necessary, by the *force publique*, posted in regional barracks. The state provided a legal framework for the companies' exploitation of Congo, defended its financial stake in the companies, and provided mail service and a rudimentary infrastructure. It did not, however, maintain a uniform rule of law or provide programs for the welfare of Congolese peoples, belying the justifications for European intervention pronounced at the Berlin Conference in 1884–1885.

Congolese peoples experienced the Congo Free State's rule in different ways. Much depended on a village's proximity to a government post, company station, mission station, or river on which goods were transported. In all such places, the demands on local labor were high. Much also depended on the kind of labor required to extract a given resource. The collection of palm oil from palm groves was less arduous than the collection of copal, a fossilized resin buried in marshes, which Europeans converted into varnish for rail carriages and furniture. Within the sovereign borders of the Congo Free State, the regime's presence was uneven. It is noteworthy that Leopold's arrogation of vacant lands was so fiercely opposed by private commercial interests that the Congo Free State exempted the lower river and the Kasai region from this monopolistic system until 1902. In the Kasai, the Kuba kingdom was virtually unaffected by the Congo Free State until the state decisively conquered it in 1899–1900.[38] In the eastern Congo, following the defeat of the last major Zanzibari forces in 1894, the Congo Free State largely appropriated the Zanzibaris' system of exploitation, even employing many of the same intermediaries and servants.[39] (See Document 9.) The Mbole people, ostensibly freed from the Zanzibaris by the Congo Free State, referred to the Europeans and their auxiliaries as Atama-Atama, a variation on the Mboles' name for the previous slave traders.[40] Throughout the state, demand for goods and labor provoked both small and large rebellions; even the African soldiers of the *force publique* sometimes revolted against their white officers. (See Document 10.)

The worst abuses were concentrated in the middle of the Congo Free State, under the authority of the concessionaire companies, which reaped huge profits as the demand for rubber grew in Europe and the United States in the 1890s. For example, the rubber boom increased ABIR's profits from 131,340 francs between 1892 and 1894 to 2,482,697 francs in 1898.[41] Tragically, this boom inspired the company and its agents to build a brutal, unsustainable system of rubber extraction on the backs of Congolese peoples.

The rubber came from landolphia vines that grew wild in the forests. To gather the rubber, a worker made an incision in a vine, and then waited for the rubber to drip into a pot. The rubber was then dried and delivered to the company agent. This process was utterly destructive of Congolese peoples for several reasons. First, the vines were quickly exhausted by regular tapping, forcing individuals to travel greater distances, foraging as best they could, to find more vines. Second, people were not adequately compensated for their labor, at the same time that rubber collection took them away from other necessary work in their villages. Third, company agents were encouraged to increase their collection of rubber without any consideration of long-term consequences. In addition to a base salary, agents earned a 2 percent commission on the rubber they collected. Each agent was given a quota, and if he failed to meet the quota, the difference was deducted from his commission. The agent in turn gave each worker a quota of rubber to collect within a fortnight.[42] The enforcement of this quota was the job of African sentries, who were employed by the companies and posted in the villages. These sentries were armed, subject to minimal oversight, and ultimately backed by the *force publique*.

To sustain the collection of rubber, agents and their sentries resorted to terror. Sentries kept women related to local men captive in a "hostage house" until the men produced the required amount of rubber. Within and outside the hostage house, sentries raped women as a matter of course. Both men and women were whipped, tortured, and murdered. The Congolese gave agents telling nicknames, such as Mpimbo Mingi (much whipping), Tumba Lombe (home burner), and Liboma (he who kills).[43] Sentries also engaged in a gruesome practice of mutilating men, women, and children, most often by severing a hand. (See Document 11.) The severed hands allegedly served as a means through which sentries accounted for expended rifle cartridges when they reported to European officials. These officials presumably wanted proof that sentries were using their weapons to coerce people into labor rather than to hunt wild game. There was actually a variety of accounts of the motives and methods of mutilation, but the collective effect was terror. This ferocious system produced great profits for the companies and the Congo Free State over a short period of time. Not only did the state own half of ABIR stock, but it also collected an annual tax of 2 percent of ABIR profits and exacted an export duty of 0.5 franc per kilo of rubber. In 1900, payments from ABIR comprised about 10 percent of the Congo Free State's total revenue.[44]

The Congolese resisted this brutal regime in two main ways. They moved, often as whole villages, out of the range of a given government or company station. (See Document 14.) They also burned stations and attacked European agents and African sentries whose actions had become intolerable. Wary of the Europeans' firepower, Congolese sometimes ambushed their adversaries, as in January 1893, when two elders joined two agents of the Anonymous Belgian Company for a walk near the company post at Basankusu on the Lopori River. According to an oral history of this incident, the elders saw a bird and, suspecting that the agents were unarmed, asked one of the agents to shoot it for them. After the agent checked his pockets and did not find his pistol, the elders killed both agents in reprisal for the agents' brutality. (See Document 12.) Sometimes fighting would erupt quickly in disputes between sentries and villagers, even as rubber was being weighed or people were being paid. (See Document 13.) A series of reprisals between villagers and company agents and sentries could result in widespread violence, or what local people called a "rubber war." (See Documents 12 and 14.) One such war resulted in the massacre of Mbandaka Wajiko, a village located south of the capital of the Equateur District, Coquilhatville (now Mbandaka) in 1896. The former servant of a district commissioner recalled, "So many people were killed that blood was one meter high; it came up to the thighs." (See Document 11.)

By 1904, virtually all the landolphia vines had been destroyed, making the agents' and sentries' ongoing demands for rubber impossible to fulfill. By 1905, both ABIR and the Company of Antwerp faced open rebellion and social collapse throughout their territories, aggravated by famines in communities already thrown into disorder. In the first six months of 1905, ABIR reported that 142 sentries had been killed or wounded by local villagers.[45] A year later, on September 12, 1906, the companies turned over their operations to the Congo Free State, which proved no more successful in reviving the collection of rubber.

Numerous Europeans in Congo, especially missionaries, observed marked declines in the indigenous population. The largest concentrations of people were to be found on the savannas to the north and south of the rain forests of the central basin, and in the eastern basin, where people practiced mixed agriculture and kept livestock.[46] The population estimates for Congo in the late nineteenth and early twentieth centuries are uncertain but significant. They are uncertain because there was no reliable census, and they are significant because estimates of the decline in population have been treated as a measure of the evil efficacy of the Congo Free State. Contemporary critics of the state charged that the regime caused the deaths of ten million people and reduced the total population of Congo by half. Recent scholarship suggests that there were probably fewer than ten million people living in the territory of the Congo Free State when it was founded in 1885 and that the population by 1908 had declined by less than a quarter—still a catastrophic loss. Most deaths were attributable not to war and atrocity, but to hunger, malnutrition, and disease, slower-moving killers let loose by European conquest and rule.[47]

The Congo Free State has been treated as an extraordinary betrayal of the principles of the Berlin Act. The depredations of the state have been characterized as genocide. However justifiable these assessments may be, they should not distract us from the fact that the state was in some respects typical of most European imperial administrations in Africa—a point the Congo Free State commonly asserted in its own defense. All European regimes in Africa sanctioned coercive systems of labor mobilization to control the transition from slavery to wage labor in their territories.[48] They generally seized African lands and imposed a variety of taxes designed to force Africans to work in the "public interest"—that is, for the benefit of the European state, private businesses, or missionaries. Acknowledging that Africans continued to work under conditions analogous to slavery, imperial officials explained that discipline and administrative control would facilitate the adaptation of "savages" to civilized cultures and economies. It would lead to "moral and material improvement." Even concessionaire companies, responsible for many of the atrocities under the Congo Free State, were by no means extraordinary institutions in this era of empire. They were also used in the French Congo and French Equatorial Africa, by the Portuguese in Mozambique, and by the Germans in Cameroon.[49]

THE CONGO REFORM CAMPAIGN

European missionaries began corresponding privately about forced labor and the abusive practices of the Congo Free State soon after its founding. By the mid-1890s, missionaries, merchants, and British consular officials based in Angola had all documented massacres and atrocities perpetrated against Congolese peoples by the state, and some had privately protested even to the secretary of state of Congo, Edmond van Eetvelde. Three of the four oral histories by Congolese peoples in this collection refer to missionaries witnessing atrocities and writing in protest to government officials, with some positive effect. Yet missionaries, merchants, and British officials all had particular interests that prompted them to mute their public criticism. Missionaries regarded the conversion of Africans to Christianity as their priority, and they worried that if they publicly embarrassed the Congo Free State, it would refuse to grant them additional station sites upriver or no longer require local villages to provide them with labor and supplies. This was of special concern to Protestant missionaries, who observed that Leopold, a Catholic, favored Catholic missions.[50] Merchants, like missionaries, were reluctant to criticize the state on which they depended for transportation, security, and trading privileges. Although individual British consular officials were outraged by the brutality of the Congo Free State, the British Foreign Office had no interest in intervening in Congo, a place of no consequence in terms of British foreign and imperial policies.

On November 18, 1895, *The Times* of London published an indictment of the Congo Free State by the Reverend John Murphy of the American Baptist Missionary Union (ABMU), who was stationed on the upper river at Bolenge. (See Document 15.) British humanitarians subsequently treated this as the first reliable, firsthand public condemnation of the state by a known author. Murphy recounted forced labor, punitive expeditions, hostage taking, and, most shocking of all, African sentries severing the hands of dead and living victims to present to their European officers. "These hands," he wrote, "the hands of men, women, and children, are placed in rows before the commissaire [a state official], who counts them to see that the soldiers have not wasted" their ammunition. Murphy further observed state officials participating in the sale of Congolese peoples as slaves, despite the Congo Free State's condemnation of slave trading by Zanzibaris. Murphy concluded, "These wretched slaves soon find they have only changed masters."

Over the next couple of years, other missionaries, such as a Swedish member of the ABMU, E. V. Sjöblom, came forward to condemn the state for slavery and other atrocities. (See Document 16.) They were mainly motivated by the fact that the chaos wrought by the state made it impossible for them to proselytize. The state refuted these charges, generally sticking to an argument introduced by Governor-General Théophile Wahis in a letter published in *The Times* on May 31, 1897, in refutation of Sjöblom. (See Document 17.) He denied that there was evidence to support the missionary's charges; he denied that the state sanctioned the severing of hands; he accused missionaries of inciting unrest among the Congolese; he assailed the character of individual missionary critics such as Sjöblom and interpreted the silence of the majority of their missionary brethren as an indication of support for the regime.

Future defenders of the Congo Free State added that missionaries depended on the state for Congolese labor and were thus complicit in any alleged exploitation. Moreover, missionaries themselves had paid to "redeem" slaves and then allegedly used these freed people as servants on their stations. Defenders of the Congo Free State also pointed to evidence of the state's work on behalf of the same civilizing mission advocated by missionaries. In 1905, for example, Henry Wellington Wack, a defender of the state, published *The Story of the Congo Free State*, in which he reproduced a circular sent to officers of the state in 1897 that instructed them to end indigenous "barbarous customs" such as witch hunts and human sacrifice. (See Document 18.) Finally, with Leopold's financial support, propagandists launched a European-wide campaign to highlight the parallels between administrative policies in Congo and those of other European imperial regimes, particularly Great Britain, in other parts of Africa. (See Document 19.)

Within several years of the first public accusations against the Congo Free State, British radicals treated the state as a tragically ironic exemplar of all that was wrong with the new imperialism. John Hobson, in his work *Imperialism: A Study* (1902), condemned the regime for exploiting the rhetoric of the civilizing mission in order to satisfy its greed through savage methods. (See Document 20.) Hobson compared injustices in Congo to the effects of the new imperialism in other parts of Africa and Asia. He charged that the civilizing mission was being undermined by belligerent nationalisms in Europe and that Europe's foreign and imperial policies had been effectively bought by private financiers and businessmen, who now manipulated elected politicians to serve their own interests in profit. It was apparent that Leopold had taken advantage of nationalist rivalries and fear of war in Africa to gain control over Congo. Moreover, Leopold had cooperated with financiers to abolish free trade in Congo and create monopolies for the unregulated exploitation of its lands and peoples. Yet members of parliament in Belgium and Britain were generally silent — proof, critics charged, of their deference to their financial masters. Hobson's views resembled those of the leading Belgian critic of the Congo Free State, the socialist Émile Vandervelde, and the leading British critic, Edmund Dene Morel. (See Document 21.) The Congo Free State thus played into a larger radical argument that imperialism undermined democracy and that brutality abroad would undermine the moral conviction of civilization at home. Civilization would thus degenerate into a civilized savagery.

Popular public protest against the Congo Free State began in Britain after Leopold and his associates had made their greatest profits and as the rubber boom in Congo came to an end. The Congo controversy arose in Britain after the British government published a report by a consular official named Roger Casement in February 1904. (See Document 22.) Having investigated conditions in the Congo Free State over the course of several months, Casement confirmed the major accusations made against the state by missionaries and merchants, and he offered transcripts of interviews with Congolese men and women. In light of this report, a coalition of missionaries, humanitarians, and merchants formed the Congo Reform Association (CRA), under the leadership of Morel, a man with strong ties to British traders and businesses in west and central Africa.

Over the next nine years, the CRA lobbied the British government to exert diplomatic pressure on Leopold to reform his regime.[51] Morel, the CRA's main publicist, argued that the welfare of Congolese peoples depended on respecting the "elementary rights of human beings."[52] He asserted specifically that respecting rights to land and the fruits of one's own labor would enable Congolese peoples and Europeans to benefit mutually in the imperial economy. (See Document 21.) He published widely and solicited the support of leading public figures, but the CRA's campaign lost momentum in 1905 and ran low on funds. The campaign was revived that summer by two English missionaries, the Reverend John and Alice Harris, members of the Congo Balolo Mission, who returned to Great Britain after working in Congo for most of the previous seven years. The Harrises reached out to British religious leaders and organizations, which exercised significant political power at this time, and developed a nationwide series of lantern slide lectures and a network of CRA auxiliaries that established a solid base of public support for the organization and stabilized its finances.

The photographic image of atrocity was a central feature of the CRA's lantern slide lectures, delivered most often by former missionaries in churches and municipal halls. The photographs were presented as definitive proof of wrongdoing and suffering. Their validity was reinforced by the testimonies of missionaries. Among the most prominent atrocity photographs was that of a boy named Epondo, who testified to Casement that his hand had been chopped off by a sentry. (See Document 23.) The missionary photographer had instructed Epondo to wrap a white cloth around his body, probably both to observe British rules of modesty and to highlight the absence of the boy's hand. Epondo, like other such photographic subjects, gazes forward in a staid yet shocking variation on contemporary portraiture. The significance of this and other atrocity photographs was defined by a narrative that led the audience through an introduction to Congo and the moral promise of the Berlin Act, the betrayals and brutalities of the Congo Free State, and the prospect of moral redemption should Britain successfully persuade or compel the state to reform its brutal practices. The CRA's speakers advocated the traditional religious principles of the civilizing mission, with additional emphasis on commerce as the guarantor of the "elementary rights of humanity." On the basis of lantern slide lectures and Morel's relentless campaign through the press and Parliament, the Congo reformers represented the Congo Free State as an iconoclastic assault on the same civilizing mission it had been meant to serve. (See Document 24.) They sustained the largest humanitarian campaign in British imperial politics before the First World War and stoked debate within Belgium itself.

In 1905, the Congo Free State authorized a commission of inquiry to travel to Congo and assess the allegations of Casement's report, as well as those of missionary critics. Upon hearing numerous testimonies from Congolese peoples, state and company employees, and missionaries, the commission produced a relatively balanced report that found specific, grave problems in the state's systems of taxation and law enforcement.

It also praised the state for exerting a civilizing influence on the presumably savage Congolese peoples through economic development and social reform programs, including the prosecution of individuals for alleged acts of cannibalism and superstition. (See Document 25.) Recognizing the power of atrocity photographs, the commission noted that in its own investigation Epondo had said that his hand had been bitten off by a wild boar. More commonly, defenders of the Congo Free State asserted that atrocity photographs had been doctored, charges that the Congo reformers denied with success in Britain and with mixed results in Belgium. In response to the commission's report and mounting protest in Britain, the Belgian parliament held a five-day debate on Congo in February and March 1906. (See Document 26.) The majority of its members agreed that reforms were necessary, but few were prepared to denounce the Congo Free State and impugn the reputation of their monarch. Defenders of the regime held sway, declaring that Belgium's duty to civilize Congo would be ultimately fulfilled.

THE BELGIAN CONGO

As the Congo reform campaign peaked in Britain in 1907 and 1908, and as scandal over the Congo atrocities grew in the international press, the British Foreign Office finally began to make pointed criticisms of the Congo Free State and demand that Leopold enact reforms. The Belgian government was not concerned about any economic leverage Britain might exercise against it. However, this was an era of rising tensions between the European great powers, driven by industrialization and arms races. Looking eastward toward the threat of Germany, the Belgian government, Leopold included, understood that Belgium's security as a neutral country was ensured by Britain under the terms of a nineteenth-century treaty. Stern words from the British government were not sufficient, however. Negotiations to transfer sovereignty over Congo from Leopold to the elected Belgian government were provoked by various factors: the British government's pressure, the indignity of international scandal, the decline in the profits of the Congo Free State, suspicion by members of the Belgian parliament that Leopold had engaged in financial improprieties, and the Belgian parliament's desire finally to assert its constitutional authority over the monarchy. The process was completed by Belgium's annexation of Congo on November 15, 1908. Leopold subsequently ordered that most of the Congo Free State's records be burned.

Under the so-called colonial charter, the Belgian government undertook major reforms of the administration of Congo to eliminate the worst abuses of the Congo Free State and put the imperial economy on a solid footing. The Belgian parliament assumed authority over the budgets of the Congo government, which was also overseen by a minister of colonies, who was himself overseen by a colonial council appointed by both the parliament and the king.[53] The most important reforms involved tax rates, currency, and trade. On January 1, 1909, the new government fixed the rate of taxation, and in the summer of 1910 it established the franc as the only legal tender in most of Congo. These two measures effectively eliminated the arbitrary levies on labor and goods that had plagued Congolese peoples under the Congo Free State. Over the course of several years, the government also divested itself from private enterprises and promoted free trade, which also reduced abuses. Finally, the government systematically extended its reach for the first time to the upper Congo River.[54] The new Belgian government of Congo remained a foreign regime bent on the exploitation of Congo and the subjugation of its peoples by force. Nonetheless, most Congolese were arguably better off than they had been under the Congo Free State.

This era of reform was marked by greater openness to international observation. In 1911, the Belgian government permitted John and Alice Harris to return to the upper Congo, where they traveled for almost eight months, covering some five thousand miles, on a fact-finding mission. In a report to the British consul at Boma, John Harris verified that systematic abuses and atrocities had come to an end, though there were still incidents of terrible violence. He warned that three features of the regime could lead it back to savagery. He noted that financiers and businessmen still enjoyed too much influence over government policies, that forced labor for the government's "public works" remained prevalent, and that the government had yet to recognize Congolese peoples' land rights. He also observed that the government was doing virtually nothing to stop what he called "native slavery"—that is, slavery among Congolese peoples themselves—which had allegedly been one of the main reasons for European intervention in Congo in the first place. (See Document 27.) The CRA in Britain continued, in lackluster fashion, to expose the shortcomings of the Belgian government in Congo and expressed reservations when the British government formally recognized it in 1913, on the strength of positive consular reports. The Congo reform campaign was brought to a formal close in London in June of that year with a declaration of victory by Morel that rang hollow in the ears of those who saw a civilizing mission far from complete. Still, the reformers recognized that there was no public support for a campaign against old or new slaveries in Congo, certainly not in view of the rising specter of war in Europe. One year later, in 1914, Europe descended into war, and

Britain rallied to a new humanitarian crisis in Belgium itself following allegations of atrocities perpetrated against the Belgian people by the advancing German army.

CONCLUSION

What do the Congo Free State and the Congo reform campaign tell us about the new imperialism? They tell us that the new imperialism was, in fact, largely driven by the oldest desires of European imperial expansion—by "gold, God, and glory," as historians have long summed up the motives of the Spanish conquistadors in the sixteenth-century Americas. Europeans, and particularly Leopold II, likewise sought to make their fortunes in Congo, drawn not by gold but by ivory, then rubber. Missionaries traveled to Congo to spread the word of their God and convert the Congolese peoples to Christianity, lending to imperial financiers, merchants, and government officials the salutary discourse of the civilizing mission. There was also the search for glory, whether by the missionary David Livingstone, in seeking a riverain "highway" into central Africa; by the unsung journalist Henry Stanley, in solving one of the great geographical questions of his age; or by the monarch Leopold II, in seeking an empire to suit his visions of personal and national grandeur. What made this era of imperialism new, from the standpoint of Europeans, was the engine of industrial capitalism, as well as technological advances that dramatically increased the speed of transportation and the scale of violence on the imperial frontier of sub-Saharan tropical Africa.

In contrast, for Congolese peoples, especially those in the upper Congo, this imperial era may have begun as something not new but seemingly familiar—with the spirits of ancestors returned from a land beneath the sea. As the Congolese found that these spirits were flesh and blood, and insatiable in their greed, they undoubtedly recognized the newness and danger of their situation. The Congo Free State demanded of its Congolese subjects new political loyalties, new economies, and new terms of labor. It imposed new systems of taxation, backed by sentries and soldiers. Although for many decades Congo had been linked to global trade networks, this new, coercive imperial economy could not be reconciled with existing local economies, because it appropriated the labor on which those economies depended. Many Congolese peoples adapted as best they could to the new imperial reality in order to sustain their livelihoods, protect the lives of families and villages, and maintain what remained of peace. Many others moved or fought, but spears and arrows were no match for rifles, and rebellions left no time to plant or harvest, to hunt or fish. At the same time, for all its military superiority, the Congo Free State lacked the power and will necessary to establish an effective administration with which to deter rebellion, because its interest in administration was never as great as its interest in profit. From the standpoint of the Congolese, the state's civilizing mission ensured only that the price of rebellion would be terribly high.

NOTES

[1] Robert Harms, *River of Wealth, River of Sorrow: The Central Zaire Basin in the Era of the Slave and Ivory Trade, 1500–1891* (New Haven, Conn.: Yale University Press, 1981), 113–14.

[2] William A. Hance, *The Geography of Modern Africa*, 2nd ed. (New York: Columbia University Press, 1975), 315.

[3] Byron Farwell, *The Man Who Presumed: A Biography of Henry M. Stanley* (New York: W. W. Norton, 1989), 101.

[4] Jan Vansina, *Being Colonized: The Kuba Experience in Rural Congo, 1880–1960* (Madison: University of Wisconsin Press, 2010), 37–38; Harms, *River of Wealth*, 210. See also Document 11.

[5] Harms, *River of Wealth*, 26–27.

[6] Vansina, *Being Colonized*, 37.

[7] Harms, *River of Wealth*, 72.

[8] Vansina, *Being Colonized*, 6.

[9] Harms, *River of Wealth*, 69.

[10] Ibid., 33–35.

[11] David Northrup, *Beyond the Bend in the River: African Labor in Eastern Zaire, 1865–1940* (Athens: Ohio University Center for International Studies, 1988), 19, 22.

[12] Much of the content of this and the next paragraph is drawn from Willy de Craemer, Jan Vansina, and Renee C. Fox, "Religious Movements in Central Africa: A Theoretical Study," *Comparative Studies in Society and History* 18, no. 4 (October 1976): 458–75.

[13] David M. Gordon, *Invisible Agents: Spirits in a Central African History* (Athens: Ohio University Press, 2012).

[14] Osumaka Likaka, *Naming Colonialism: History and Collective Memory in the Congo, 1870–1960* (Madison: University of Wisconsin Press, 2009), 93–94.

[15] Harms, *River of Wealth*, 50.

[16] Ibid., 43, 70.

[17] Ibid., 54.

[18] Ibid., 5.

[19] Ibid., 47.

[20] Vansina, *Being Colonized*, 28, 65.

[21] Harms, *River of Wealth*, 231.

[22] *Dr. Livingstone's Cambridge Lectures*, ed. Rev. William Monk (London: Deighton, Bell, 1860), 165.

[23] Kevin Grant, *A Civilised Savagery: Britain and the New Slaveries in Africa, 1884–1926* (New York: Routledge, 2005), 19.

[24] Henry Wellington Wack, *The Story of the Congo Free State* (New York: G. P. Putnam's Sons, 1905), 16.

[25] Likaka, *Naming Colonialism*, 56.

[26] Daniel R. Headrick, *The Tools of Empire* (New York: Oxford University Press, 1981), 197.

[27] H. H. Johnston, *The River Congo, from Its Mouth to Bolobo* (London: Sampson Low, Marston, Searle, & Rivington, 1884), 439.

[28]"General Act of the Conference of Berlin," 26 February 1885, in *The Map of Africa by Treaty*, 3rd ed., vol. 2, ed. Sir Edward Hertslet (1909; repr., London: Frank Cass, 1967), 473.

[29]Jean Stengers, "King Leopold's Congo, 1886–1908," in *The Cambridge History of Africa*, vol. 6, *1870–1905*, ed. Roland Oliver and G. N. Sanderson (Cambridge: Cambridge University Press, 1985), 318, 323.

[30]L. H. Gann and Peter Duignan, *The Rulers of Belgian Africa, 1884–1914* (Princeton, N.J.: Princeton University Press, 1979), 117–23.

[31]Stengers, "King Leopold's Congo," 331.

[32]Ibid., 318.

[33]Ibid., 319.

[34]Captain Guy Burrows, *The Curse of Central Africa* (London: R. A. Everett, 1903), 205.

[35]Northrup, *Beyond the Bend in the River*, 39n6.

[36]Stengers, "King Leopold's Congo," 351.

[37]Vansina, *Being Colonized*, 118.

[38]Ibid., 33.

[39]Northrup, *Beyond the Bend in the River*, 37–46.

[40]Likaka, *Naming Colonialism*, 102–5.

[41]Robert Harms, "The World ABIR Made: The Maringa-Lopori Basin, 1885–1903," *African Economic History* 22 (1983): 130–31.

[42]Robert Harms, "The End of Red Rubber: A Reassessment," *Journal of African History* 16, no. 1 (1975): 79.

[43]Likaka, *Naming Colonialism*, 88–89, 107.

[44]Harms, "The End of Red Rubber," 81.

[45]Ibid., 85.

[46]Northrup, *Beyond the Bend in the River*, 14–15.

[47]Vansina, *Being Colonized*, 144, 147.

[48]Frederick Cooper, "Conditions Analogous to Slavery: Imperialism and Free Labor Ideology in Africa," in *Beyond Slavery*, ed. Frederick Cooper, Thomas C. Holt, and Rebecca J. Scott (Chapel Hill: University of North Carolina Press, 2000), 107–56.

[49]Aldwin Roes, "Towards a History of Mass Violence in the État Indépendant du Congo, 1885–1908," *South African Historical Journal* 62, no. 4 (2010): 639n26; Birmingham/Martin, 39; Ralph A. Austen and Rita Headrick, "Equatorial Africa under Colonial Rule," in *History of Central Africa*, vol. 2, ed. David Birmingham and Phyllis M. Martin (London: Longman, 1983), 39.

[50]Stengers, "King Leopold's Congo," 346.

[51]Kevin Grant, "Christian Critics of Empire: Missionaries, Lantern Lectures, and the Congo Reform Campaign in Britain," in *The Rise and Fall of Modern Empires*, vol. 4, *Reactions to Colonialism*, ed. Martin Shipway (London: Ashgate, 2013), 91–122.

[52]E. D. Morel, "The Crisis in the Campaign against Congo Misrule" (Liverpool: Congo Reform Association, 1907), 28.

[53]Guy Vanthemsche, *Belgium and the Congo, 1885–1980* (Cambridge: Cambridge University Press, 2012), 27–28.

[54]Vansina, *Being Colonized*, 117–19.

The Documents

PART TWO

The Documents

1

DAVID LIVINGSTONE

Lecture at the University of Cambridge
December 4, 1857

David Livingstone (1813–1873) was a Scottish Congregationalist, a member of the London Missionary Society, and the most famous European missionary and explorer in Africa in the mid-nineteenth century. He gave this lecture in 1857, after completing the first coast-to-coast journey by a European across the African continent, between 1853 and 1856. Here he refers mainly to a region of central Africa located south of Congo. He recounts a journey that began in southern Africa, where he was first stationed as a missionary; proceeded north to the Portuguese coastal settlement of Luanda, in what is now Angola; and then continued east across Africa to the mouth of the Zambezi River, in what is now Mozambique. When Livingstone delivered this speech, the Congo River had not yet been mapped, although he and other explorers had begun to speculate on its course. Henry Stanley, who tracked the river twenty years later, was strongly influenced by Livingstone. Stanley first made a name for himself when he rescued Livingstone, who was stranded in central Africa, in 1871. In finally mapping the Congo River in 1877 and then using it to construct the Congo Free State, Stanley saw himself as advancing Livingstone's work. In this excerpt, Livingstone offers a concise statement of the principles and ideas widely held by Europeans regarding their exploration of Africa and of their "civilizing mission" at the outset of the era of the "new imperialism." According to Livingstone, why should Christianity and commerce be inseparable? What evidence of competition or even conflict between Livingstone and other Europeans do you see in this speech?

If you look at the map of Africa you will discover the shortness of the coast-line, which is in consequence of the absence of deep indentations of the sea. This is one reason why the interior of Africa has remained so long unknown to the rest of the world. Another reason is

---

Dr Livingstone's Cambridge Lectures, ed. Rev. William Monk (London: Deighton, Bell, 1860), 145–46, 151, 153–54, 161–63, 165.

the unhealthiness of the coast, which seems to have reacted upon the disposition of the people, for they are very unkindly, and opposed to Europeans passing through their country. . . .

My object in going into the country south of the [Kalahari] desert was to instruct the natives in a knowledge of Christianity, but many circumstances prevented my living amongst them more than seven years, amongst which were considerations arising out of the slave system carried on by the Dutch Boers [Afrikaners of southern Africa]. I resolved to go into the country beyond, and soon found that, for the purposes of commerce, it was necessary to have a path to the sea. I might have gone on instructing the natives in religion, but as civilization and Christianity must go on together, I was obliged to find a path to the sea, in order that I should not sink to the level of the natives. . . .

. . . I resolved to go to the north, and then westwards to the Portuguese settlement of Loanda [Luanda]. Along the course of the river which we passed, game was so abundant that there was no difficulty in supplying the wants of my whole party: antelopes were so tame that they might be shot from the canoe. But beyond 14 degrees of south latitude the natives had guns, and had themselves destroyed the game, so that I and my party had to live on charity. . . . When we got near the Portuguese settlement of Angola . . . payment was demanded for every thing. But I had nothing to pay with. Now the people had been in the habit of trading with the slavers, and so they said I might give one of my men in payment for what I wanted. When I shewed them that I could not do this, they looked upon me as an interloper, and I was sometimes in danger of being murdered. . . .

The people of central Africa have religious ideas stronger than those of the . . . southern nations, who talk much of God but pray seldom. They pray to departed relatives, by whom they imagine illnesses are sent to punish them for any neglect on their part. Evidences of the Portuguese Jesuit missionary operations are still extant, and are carefully preserved by the natives: one tribe can all read and write, which is ascribable to the teaching of the Jesuits: their only books are, however, histories of saints, and miracles effected by the parings of saintly toe-nails, and such-like nonsense: but, surely, if such an impression has once been produced, it might be hoped that the efforts of Protestant missionaries, who would leave the Bible with these poor people, would not be less abiding.

In a commercial point of view communication with this country is desirable. Angola is wonderfully fertile, producing every kind of tropical plant in rank luxuriance. Passing on to the valley of Quango, the stalk of the grass was as thick as a quill, and towered above my head, although I was mounted on my ox; cotton is produced in great abundance, though merely woven into common cloth; bananas and pine-apples grow in great luxuriance; but the people having no maritime communication, these advantages are almost lost. The country on the other side is not quite so fertile, but in addition to indigo, cotton, and sugar-cane, produces a fibrous substance, which I am assured is stronger than flax.

The Zambesi [Zambezi] has not been thought much of as a river by Europeans, not appearing very large at its mouth; but on going up it for about seventy miles, it is enormous. The first three hundred miles might be navigated without obstacle: then there is a rapid, and near it a coal-field of large extent. The elevated sides of the basin, which form the most important feature of the country, are far different in climate to the country nearer the sea, or even the centre. Here the grass is short, and the Angola goat, which could not live in the centre, had been seen on the east highland. . . .

My desire is to open a path to this district, that civilization, commerce, and Christianity might find their way there. I consider that we made a great mistake, when we carried commerce into India, in being ashamed of our Christianity; as a matter of common sense and good policy, it is always best to appear in one's true character. . . .

. . . The natives of Central Africa are very desirous of trading, but their only traffic is at present in slaves of which the poorer people have an unmitigated horror: it is therefore most desirable to . . . open a way for the consumption of free productions, and the introduction of Christianity and commerce. By encouraging the native propensity for trade, the advantages that might be derived in a commercial point of view are incalculable; nor should we lose sight of the inestimable blessings it is in our power to bestow upon the unenlightened African, by giving him the light of Christianity. Those two pioneers of civilization — Christianity and commerce — should ever be inseparable.

Justification

2

KING LEOPOLD II

Speech at the First Meeting of the Belgian Committee of the International Association for the Exploration and Civilization of Central Africa

November 6, 1876

In this selection, King Leopold II of Belgium (1835–1909) addresses the new international organization he founded for the abolition of the slave trade in central Africa. He was inspired to undertake this ostensibly humanitarian work by reports on Congo written by an Englishman, Lieutenant Verney Lovett Cameron, who passed through the region during his transcontinental journey between 1873 and 1875, observing abundant and potentially lucrative resources. At the beginning of this speech, Leopold refers to the slave trade in Africa as a "plague-spot that every friend of civilisation would desire to see disappear," paraphrasing the last words of David Livingstone. The missionary had observed before his death that God's blessing would fall on everyone who worked to end the slave trade in Africa and "help to heal this open sore of the world." What are the similarities and differences between Livingstone's speech in 1857 (Document 1) and this speech by Leopold in 1876? Given that Livingstone was a Scottish Protestant missionary and Leopold was a Belgian Catholic monarch who subsequently favored Catholic missions in Congo, can one argue that these men shared an understanding of the civilizing mission?

Gentlemen, . . . the slave trade, which still exists over a large part of the African Continent, is a plague-spot that every friend of civilisation would desire to see disappear.

The horrors of that traffic, the thousands of victims massacred each year through the slave trade, the still greater number of perfectly innocent beings who, brutally reduced to captivity, are condemned *en masse* to forced labour in perpetuity, have deeply moved all those who have even partially studied this deplorable situation, and concerting, in a

Henry Wellington Wack, *The Story of the Congo Free State* (New York: G. P. Putnam's Sons, 1905), 14–16.

word, for the founding of an International Association to put an end to an odious traffic which makes our epoch blush, and to tear aside the veil of darkness which still enshrouds Central Africa. The discoveries due to daring explorers permit us to say from this day that it is one of the most beautiful and the richest countries created by God.

The Conference of Brussels has nominated an Executive Committee to carry into execution its declaration and resolutions.

The Conference has wished, in order to place itself in closer relationship with the public, whose sympathy will constitute our force, to found, in each State, National Committees. These Committees, after delegating two members from each of them to form part of the International Committee, will popularise in their respective countries the adopted programme.

The work has already obtained in France and Belgium important subscriptions, which make us indebted to the donors. These acts of charity, so honourable to those who have rendered them, stimulate our zeal in the mission we have undertaken. Our first task should be to touch the hearts of the masses, and, while increasing our numbers, to gather in a fraternal union, little onerous for each member but powerful and fruitful by the accumulation of individual efforts and their results.

The International Association does not pretend to reserve for itself all the good that could or ought to be done in Africa. It ought, especially at the commencement, to forbid itself a too extensive programme. Sustained by public sympathy, we hold the conviction that, if we accomplish the opening of the routes, if we succeed in establishing stations along the routes followed by the slave merchants, this odious traffic will be wiped out, and that these routes and these stations, while serving as fulcrums for travellers, will powerfully contribute towards the evangelisation of the blacks, and towards the introduction among them of commerce and modern industry.

We boldly affirm that all those who desire the enfranchisement of the black races are interested in our success.

The Belgian Committee, emanating from the International Committee, and its representative in Belgium, will exert every means to procure for the work the greatest number of adherents. It will assist my countrymen to prove once more that Belgium is not only a hospitable soil, but that she is also a generous nation, among whom the cause of humanity finds as many champions as she has citizens.

I discharge a very agreeable duty in thanking this assembly, and in warmly congratulating it for having imposed on itself a task the accomplishment of which will gain for our country another brilliant page in the annals of charity and progress.

3

Treaty of Manyanga

August 12, 1882

This document exemplifies the many treaties through which Congolese chiefs ceded property and political and legal authority to the Committee for Studies of the Upper Congo and its nominal successor, the International Association of the Congo, both of which served Leopold II. These treaties became part of the legal foundation of the sovereignty of the Congo Free State in the eyes of other European governments. The term palabre, *which appears in the first sentence of the treaty, is now more commonly spelled* palaver *and refers to a negotiation. What are the different ways in which this treaty transferred authority from Congolese chiefs to the Committee for Studies of the Upper Congo? What benefits did the committee get under the terms of this treaty, and what benefits did Congolese peoples get? What challenges might the chiefs have faced in conducting their negotiations and in understanding the significance of the treaty?*

During the *palabre* [palaver] held at Manyanga the 12th of August, 1882, it is agreed between the members hereinafter designated of the expedition of the Upper Congo:

Dr. Edward Pecheul Loesche, chief of the Expedition;
Capt. Edmund Hanssens, chief of the division of Leopold-Manyanga;
Lieut. Arthur Niles, chief of Manyanga;
First Lieut. Orban, deputy chief of Manyanga;
Edward Ceris, assistant of Pechuel, representing the *Comité* of the
　　Upper Congo;
and the chiefs hereafter named of Manyanga—
Makito, of Kintamba;
Nkosi, of Kintamba;
Filankuni, of Kintamba;
Maluka, of Kintamba;
Kuakala, of Kintamba;
Mankatula, of Kintamba-Kimbuku;

Henry Wellington Wack, *The Story of the Congo Free State* (New York: G. P. Putnam's Sons, 1905), 488–89.

Luamba, of Kintamba;
In the name of their subjects.

ARTICLE I—Hereafter the territory of Manyanga, heretofore belonging to the chiefs before cited, situated north and south of the river, and bounded on the west by the stream Luseto, and by the stream Msua Mungua on the east, shall be the sole property of the *Comité d' Études* of the Upper Congo.

ART. II—The chiefs and their subjects, their villages, their plantations, their domestic animals, and fishing apparatus shall be placed under the protection of the Expedition.

ART. III—In all political affairs of the populations of the district protected and acquired, their quarrels, differences, elections of chiefs, shall be submitted to the decision of the member of the Expedition who shall be present at the station.

If the people of Manyanga shall be attacked by neighbouring tribes, the Expedition shall defend their women and children and their property by all the means in their power. If the Expedition shall be attacked by another tribe, the men shall be bound to defend the station.

ART. IV—In consequence of the rights acquired and protection afforded, no stranger whatsoever can build or open a road or carry on commerce in the territory of Manyanga.

ART. V—At the request of the chief of the station, the chief of the district shall put at his disposition the necessary number of labourers, men or women, for the work of the station and the service of the caravans.

ART. VI—Besides the sum stipulated, which has been remitted in goods to the assembled chiefs in payment for their territories, and for which they have given a receipt, the chiefs shall receive monthly presents on condition that they remain true friends and voluntarily perform the services asked of them.

ART. VII—The first chief of Manyanga, Makito, residing at Kintamba, receives the flag of the Expedition, which he will raise in his village in sign of the protection exercised by the Expedition.

[Here follow the crosses and signatures.]

4

HARRY JOHNSTON

From The River Congo

1884

Harry Johnston (1858–1927) was one of Britain's leading authorities on African affairs in the era of the new imperialism. He held several British consular posts in sub-Saharan Africa in the late nineteenth century, and he participated in important territorial negotiations with African rulers and European imperial powers. A prolific author, he was widely respected as a geographer, botanist, and ethnologist — what we would today call an anthropologist. He met Henry Stanley in Congo in 1883, while traveling in a private capacity, and joined Stanley in a journey by steamer above Malebo Pool (then known as Stanley Pool). This paean to the civilizing mission of Stanley and Leopold II indicates that Stanley exploited divisions between Congolese chiefs to establish the Congo Free State. Moreover, Johnston asserts that the Congolese peoples would never be able to unify and rule themselves, suggesting that the civilizing mission — at least to his mind — would never result in political independence. How does Johnston evaluate the progress of "civilization" in Congo? How does his description of the foundation of Leopold II's rule differ from the specific terms of the Treaty of Manyanga (Document 3)? What does the treaty suggest that Johnston overlooks in his account?

What has hitherto made Mr. Stanley's work so rapid and so comparatively easy has been the want of cohesion amongst the native chiefs; he has had no great jealous empire to contend with, as he would have had farther north or farther south. If one village declined to let him settle among them, the next town, out of rivalry, received him with open arms. . . . By banding the native kinglets in union — union which would inevitably turn them with race jealousy against the white man, the entry of civilisation into the Congo countries will be hindered, and this great work made dependent on the caprices of an African despot. The black

---

H. H. Johnston, *The River Congo, from Its Mouth to Bolobo* (London: Sampson Low, Marston, Searle, & Rivington, 1884), 436–39.

man, though he may make a willing subject, can never rule. These people are well disposed in their present condition to receive civilisation, but the civilisation must come not as a humble suppliant but as a monarch. It must be able to inspire respect as well as naïve wonder, and this is what the expedition as conducted by Mr. Stanley has succeeded in doing.

To realise this, let us . . . consider the state of the Congo only seven years ago, and compare it with the present state of affairs. In 1876 the European merchants had penetrated no farther than Boma, where they were all established. There was not a single trading station higher up the river. No one knew anything of the country beyond Isangila, except that the natives were all cannibals. . . .

The merchants of Boma, since Stanley's advent, have founded fifteen trading stations between Boma and the falls at Vivi. There was not a single missionary on the Congo before 1879. Now there are three flourishing missions, the Livingstone, the Baptist, and the Roman Catholic, with many stations between Stanley Pool and the sea. . . . Establishments like Vivi and Léopoldville, which deserve to be called small towns, have been created, and other stations, numbering in all some twenty-one, have been founded; so that now, between Equator Station, at the mouth of the great Mobindu, and the coast, there is a distance of over 700 miles secured to civilisation, and offering no greater risks to the traveller than those attributable to the elements or to the ordinary contrarieties of tropical rivers.

Mr. Stanley has three steamers on the Upper river and a small fleet of lighters [barges] and canoes. The native chiefs are his active coadjutors. He everywhere keeps the peace, and is looked up to as the great umpire in regions where he was once a hunted fugitive. In short, whichever way our sympathies may go — and as Englishmen we ought to sympathise with this splendid outlet thrown open to our commerce — we must at least admit that the work is a colossal one, and that the man who has undertaken it has the indomitable will of the Anglo-Saxon; nor should we fail to remember that the King of the Belgians, as President of the African International Association, has an equal share with Mr. Stanley in the gratitude and admiration of the civilised world. While there are probably few men who could have been found to cope with the difficulties and perils of this undertaking in the way that Mr. Stanley has done, so nowhere, probably, does there exist a living philanthropist like Léopold II, who could from pure love of knowledge and civilisation open up a road across Africa for the benefit of the world, and endow munificently from his private fortune an enterprise for the good of future generations.

5

General Act of the Conference of Berlin, Articles V, VI, IX, and XIII

1885

The "General Act of the Conference of Berlin," commonly known as the Berlin Act, was signed by the representatives of twelve European governments, the Ottoman emperor, and the United States on February 26, 1885. This international treaty was intended to establish rules for imperial expansion in central and west Africa in order to prevent conflict between the competing powers. The articles excerpted here outline the signatories' support of free trade, Christian missions, and the abolition of slavery. None of the signatories wished to assume the costs and challenges of establishing a government in Congo, however, so they enjoined the International Association of the Congo, controlled by Leopold II, to ensure "the equality of treatment of all nations" in trade and to advance the civilizing mission through such trade, Christian conversion, abolition, scientific research, and exploration. What are the strengths and limitations of the Berlin Act as a historical source of information about the new imperialism in Africa?

No Monopolies or Favours to be granted

Art. V.—No Power which exercises or shall exercise sovereign rights in the above-mentioned regions shall be allowed to grant therein a monopoly or favour of any kind in matters of trade.

Protection of Persons and Property, movable and immovable Possessions; Professions

Foreigners, without distinction, shall enjoy therein with regard to the protection of their persons and effects, the acquisition and transmission of their movable and real property and with regard to the exercise of their professions, the same treatment and the same rights as nationals.

"General Act of the Conference of Berlin," 26 February 1885, in *The Map of Africa by Treaty*, 3rd ed., vol. 2, ed. Sir Edward Hertslet (1909; repr., London: Frank Cass, 1967), 473–76.

ART. VI.—*Provisions relative to Protection of the Natives, of Missionaries and Travellers, as well as relative to Religious Liberty*

Preservation and Improvement of Native Tribes; Slavery, and the Slave Trade

All the Powers exercising sovereign rights or influence in the aforesaid territories bind themselves to watch over the preservation of the native tribes, and to care for the improvement of the conditions of their moral and material well-being, and to help in suppressing slavery, and especially the slave trade.

Religious and other Institutions; Civilization of Natives

They shall, without distinction of creed or nation, protect and favour all religions, scientific, or charitable institutions; and undertakings created and organized for the above ends, or which aim at instructing the natives and bringing home to them the blessings of civilization.

Protection of Missionaries, Scientists, and Explorers

Christian missionaries, scientists and explorers, with their followers, property, and collections, shall likewise be the objects of especial protection.

Religious Toleration

Freedom of conscience and religious toleration are expressly guaranteed to the natives, no less than to subjects and to foreigners.

Public Worship

The free and public exercise of all forms of Divine worship, and the right to build edifices for religious purposes, and to organize religious missions belonging to all creeds, shall not be limited or fettered in any way whatsoever. . . .

Suppression of the Slave Trade by Land and Sea; and of Slave Markets

ART. IX.—Seeing that trading in slaves is forbidden in conformity with the principles of international law as recognized by the Signatory Powers, and seeing also that the operations, which, by sea or land, furnish slaves to trade, ought likewise to be regarded as forbidden, the Powers which do or shall exercise sovereign rights or influence in the territories forming the Conventional basin of the Congo declare that these territories may not serve as a market or means of transit for the trade in slaves, of whatever race they may be. Each of the Powers binds itself to employ all the means at its disposal for putting an end to this trade and for punishing those who engage in it. . . .

The Congo and its Branches open to the Merchant Vessels of all Nations

ART. XIII.—The navigation of the Congo, without excepting any of its branches or outlets, is, and shall remain, free for the merchant ships of all nations equally, whether carrying cargo or ballast, for the transport of goods or passengers. It shall be regulated by the provisions of this Act of Navigation, and by the Rules to be made in pursuance thereof.

Equality of Treatment to all Nations; Coasting Trade; Boat Traffic

In the exercise of this navigation the subjects and flags of all nations shall in all respects be treated on a footing of perfect equality, not only for the direct navigation from the open sea to the inland ports of the Congo and *vice versa*, but also for the great and small coasting trade, and for boat traffic on the course of the river. . . .

International Law

These provisions are recognized by the Signatory Powers as becoming henceforth a part of international law.

6

WALTER DEANE

Account of the Destruction of the Congo Free State's Station at Stanley Falls in an Attack by Zanzibari Slave Traders

1886

Walter Deane was the chief of the Congo Free State's station at Stanley Falls (now Boyoma Falls) when it fell to Zanzibari ivory and slave traders in 1886. Prior to his death two years later, Deane described the attack to Herbert Ward, who published the account in his book Five Years with the Congo Cannibals *in 1891. Deane refers to the Zanzibaris as "Arabs," but they were, in fact, Swahili-speaking Muslims from the sultanate of Zanzibar, off the coast of East Africa. He also refers to Manyemas, a Bantu-speaking indigenous people employed by the Zanzibaris. The station at Stanley Falls, located in the eastern Congo basin, was a distant outpost of the newly founded Congo Free State, located in territory still dominated by the Zanzibaris. After the station fell, the Congo Free State employed the most powerful slave trader in central Africa, Tippu Tip, to serve as the governor of the Stanley Falls District, a position he held for the next three or four years. What does this account tell you about the organization and power of the Congo Free State in its early years?*

Upon my arrival, I found things in a very bad condition, that the Arabs had the entire upper hand, and bullied the natives just as they pleased; yet I could do nothing to prevent them, for it was too far off, the time of my expected re-inforcements, to provoke any conflict then. . . .

. . . At last, *Le Stanley* was signaled, early one morning, coming up the river, and I was indeed delighted, for I expected she would have on board the much needed ammunition and re-inforcements. But imagine my disgust . . . when, on getting to the landing-place, I found she had not

Herbert Ward, *Five Years with the Congo Cannibals* (London: Chatto & Windus, 1891), 196–97, 202, 205–10.

brought me a single cartridge of the promised ten thousand—not a rifle, and not a man, save only Lieutenant Dubois, of the Belgian Lancers. He turned out to be a splendid fellow; but still I needed the other things, or my fight was hopeless. . . .

. . . Toward evening, I was told by a friendly native that the Arabs intended attacking the station the following morning. . . . At dawn we found, sure enough, a large party of Manyemas had crossed from the mainland in the night, and had intrenched themselves on my island, about eight hundred yards from the stockade. As soon as it was light, we received a practical proof of their hostility, for they fired upon us. We kept up a lively fire upon them for two days with our Snyder and Martini rifles, but they were well sheltered by their rough earthworks, and there were no serious losses on either side.

Our men kept up a tremendous fusilade whenever the Arabs made any signs of attacking, and, on the evening of the third day, Dubois sallied out of the stockades and penetrated into the Arab lines, capturing a Manyema drum which they left in their flight. It was hot work, and he got his revolver pouch shot off his hip. That night they remained quiet, but in the morning fresh earth heaps were found thrown up nearer our intrenchments, and the fight recommenced. Our ammunition was now beginning to fail, and so we could not waste so many shots, and the Arabs took advantage of this to make two or three rushes right up to our position; but we drove them back each time, and I worked the Krupps [cannon] so hard that blood came from my ears, and I knocked the end off my little finger by getting it jammed in the breech. . . . Dubois charged out again and drove them back, and then darkness set in and stopped the fight for the night. The Bangalas [members of a Congolese people employed by the state] deserted that night, taking some native canoes, and making off down river to try and reach Bangala, which you know is a five hundred miles' journey.

In the morning the fight started again. We could now do little but work the Krupps, as the little rifle ammunition we had left was almost entirely bad. We got cap guns and old trade flint-locks out of the store and gave them to the Houssas [West African soldiers] to fire; but seven of these poor chaps were already dead, and the rest, all save Musa Kanu and three men, came to me in the evening and said they must go; that it was no use fighting when they were bound to fall into the hands of the Arabs. I threatened to shoot them as deserters, and they replied:

"Very well, master, you shoot us; we would rather you shoot us than have our throats cut by the Arabs."

And as soon as darkness set in, they made off to the canoes and drifted down river after the Bangalas.

Dubois and I were now left with only four Houssas and Samba, a native of the Aruimi [Aruwimi], who had been freed by the State, and worked faithfully with me during all my stay at the Falls, and despairingly we determined to destroy that night all that we could of the stores remaining, to spike the guns, and blow up the station, and make off to the woods, to hide until relief should come from Bangala, where we reckoned the fugitive Bangalas would arrive by a certain date, and Coquilhat would hurry up in the steamer *A.I.A.* (*Association Internationale Africaine*) to our relief. We sprinkled the stores with oil, piled up the cartridges, spiked the Krupps, and gathered all the loose gunpowder together; and having set a train to this outside the station, we two, with Musa Kanu and his three faithful Houssas, and Samba, who refused to budge without us, made off under cover of the darkness, to gain the north shore and seek shelter in the woods there.

I was the last to leave the place, and I set fire to the train of powder and made after the rest. . . .

The night was pitch dark and the station was blazing behind us, but somehow the gunpowder had not exploded. We knew the Arabs must have discovered our flight by this time, so we hurried along to cross over to the mainland. We had to wade through an arm of the Congo, a rushing torrent of water about fifty yards wide, and generally at that season only waist deep. Dubois slipped on the rocks and was swept down into deeper water. . . . By the light of the burning station, where the cartridges and gunpowder had now commenced to explode, illuminating vividly for the moment the surrounding scene, I searched the waters for any sign of poor Dubois, but alas, poor fellow, . . . he had been swept away by the current. It was the last I ever saw of him, and my grief and misery were so great at the loss of my only friend away up there, after all the pluck he had shown during the four days' fighting at the station, that I wept, while the Houssas, after pulling me up, cried too.

We were, indeed, a wretched lot. My clothes had been burnt off me and torn in the fight. I had only an old blanket around me and a shirt on, and no boots; and sadly, and feeling that I didn't care if the Arabs should find me and end the wretchedness at once, I crept away into the forest.

7

TIPPU TIP

From Autobiography

Tippu Tip (1837–1905) was the most powerful slave trader between the eastern Congo and Zanzibar in the late nineteenth century. He worked for the sultan of Zanzibar for many years, amassing great wealth and gaining a transcontinental reputation as a shrewd, ruthless business-man. At a critical stage of Henry Stanley's exploration of central Africa, Tippu Tip joined him, offering protection and guidance for several weeks. After the fall of the Congo Free State station at Stanley Falls in 1886 (see Document 6), Stanley enlisted Tippu Tip to serve as the governor of the Stanley Falls District between 1887 and 1890 or 1891. The following excerpt from Tippu Tip's autobiography has two parts. The first part recounts his meeting with Stanley and their journey through and beyond the slave-trading entrepôt at Nyangwe. Bear in mind that Tippu Tip was a Muslim and Stanley was a Christian, an "Unbeliever," with whom a Muslim should presumably not travel. The second part of the document recounts the negotiation between Stanley and Tippu Tip in Zanzibar that resulted in the latter's governorship of Stanley Falls. This is followed by Tippu Tip's summary of how he transformed the station into a thriving market for ivory. How do these accounts by Tippu Tip affect your inter-pretation of previous documents in this collection? Was it possible for the Congo Free State to hire Tippu Tip and still viably claim that it was working to abolish slavery and promote free trade and Christian missions in Congo?

A month passed there until one afternoon Stanley appeared. We greeted him, welcomed him and gave him a house. The following morning we went to see him and he showed us a gun, telling us, "From this gun 15 bullets come out!" Now we knew of no such gun firing 15 rounds, nei-ther knew of one nor had seen such. I asked him, "From a single bar-rel?" He said they came from a single barrel, so I asked him to fire it so

Maisha ya Hamed bin Muhammed el Murjebi yaani Tippu Tip, *Autobiography*, introduc-tion by Miss Alison Smith, trans. W. H. Whiteley, *Supplement to the East African Swahili Committee Journals*, no. 28/2 (July 1958) and no. 29/1 (January 1959), 111, 113, 151, 153, 159.

that we could see. . . . How could the bullets come out of one barrel, one after another? I said to him, "Over in Rumami there's a bow which takes twenty arrows. When you fire, all twenty fly together. And each arrow kills a man." At that he went outside and fired twelve rounds. Then he took a pistol and fired six rounds. He came back and sat down on the verandah. We were amazed. I asked him how he loaded the bullets and he showed me.

Two days passed; on the third he asked me whether I knew Munza. I said, "I neither know Munza nor have I ever heard of the country called Munza." He told me, "If you go to Nyangwe and go north for thirty days you'll get to Munza. Look here, you seem to me to be the right sort of person, and I'd like you to take me." I agreed tentatively. "Furthermore," he said, "I'll give you 7,000 dollars." I told him that I wouldn't take him for the sake of 7,000 dollars and showed him the ivory I had. "I shall go from good-will and it won't be 7,000 dollars that seduces me from here." Stanley was amazed at the quantity of ivory: I told him I would give him my considered answer in the morning. I slept, and on the following morning told him I would agree to take him. On the second day we set off . . . and reached Nyangwe. There, people were more outspoken in trying to dissuade me, and derided me, "What, going with a European, have you lost your senses? You're mad, will you then become a European? Yet you're not needy, why then? You have your stock of ivory, why then follow an Unbeliever?" I told them, "Maybe I am mad, and you that are sensible, keep to your own affairs."

We left Nyangwe, and went north through the forest where one cannot see the sun for the size of the trees, except in the clearings for cultivation or villages. We were in difficulties because of the mud[,] particularly those who were carrying the boats. Night came, and we slept; the boats were benighted on the road. This was a blow for the men carrying Stanley's loads and the boat. One day's journey took three days. Stanley was in despair, he said to me, "What do you suggest? This trouble is serious, what do you say? How many days to the Congo?" I said to him, "We've never been, but it is not far; in six or seven days we should arrive. It is the forest that is the difficulty, but the river is near." He urged us to press on to the river.

When we got to the river we saw some locals coming with their tiny dug-outs, two men to each vessel. They came quite close to us and we called them but they shouted abuses at us. Stanley was particularly pleased to arrive at the river and set about assembling the boat. The locals came up close, and we called them, but again they shouted abuses at us and asked us what we were doing. We replied that we were making wato, that is to say dug-outs. We went on until the boat was finished. Stanley and I boarded the boat together with Abdallah bin Abed, my servant; two of my slaves, and fourteen of Stanley's men, making a total in all of eighteen men. The small dug-outs of the locals numbered more than three hundred. We fired several rounds, and they were filled with alarm. They were called WaGenia and spent their lives fishing. Some gave themselves up, and left their canoes, of which we seized more than thirty and with which we crossed the river.

Their villages they build near the river; we saw just the empty villages, the villagers had fled. For the most part their food was bananas, and their goats were very numerous. We seized several of these. We stayed on the far bank and despatched the boat to ferry over our men to the bank on which we were—where the villages were also. . . .

. . . I was in Zanzibar for two months until news came that Mr. D. [Walter Deane] who was in Stanley Falls, had been in conflict with the Arabs and had fled.

During the third month, Stanley appeared, with some ten other Europeans; we met at the Consul's. Mr. H. told me, "We wanted the expedition to come direct to the West coast from Europe, but when I heard that you were in Zanzibar, we decided to come to see you for two reasons. Firstly, we wanted you to be Wali [governor] of the Belgian area, and your men in these areas to raise the Belgian flag. Secondly we want you to give us men to [rescue] Emin Pasha [a European official then beseiged near Lake Albert]." I replied that I must communicate with Seyyid Barghash [Sultan of Zanzibar], since both we ourselves and our areas were under his authority. They replied that all authority was in my hands, and that the areas of Manyema were under my control; that I was, in fact, the chief. They wrote down a contract and Mr. H. read it out to me.

I took it to Seyyid and told him all that had passed. Seyyid advised me to go, and to go as far as they wanted. I complained to him about the wage they were giving me, thirty pounds a month. But he maintained I should go even for ten pounds a month, and I would still be able to carry on my business.

We stayed three days and set off, myself and a hundred men of mine. I instructed Muhammed bin Masud el Wardi to send on to Manyema goods to the value of 30,000 dollars. On leaving Zanzibar, Stanley and I made our farewells to Seyyid Barghash. He gave Stanley a diamond ring and a scimitar; to me he gave a diamond ring and a gold watch; also 2,000 rupees. . . .

We stayed on in Stanley Falls. Every month Europeans came to the camp, two or three boat loads and they all left with a load of ivory. Some they left behind. Stanley Falls was full of Europeans and as many goods as you could want. It became a great harbour. Anything you wanted was available. A company of Belgian and French contractors arrived; they governed the towns — God's Blessing on them! All the boats that arrived took on a cargo of ivory. On another occasion, the Belgian Governor arrived who was anxious to establish a tax on ivory. On each frasila [a unit of weight], five pounds to the State and thirty for the owner. I agreed with this saying, "For my own I will give you the five, but for the other Arabs take three only per frasila." They acquiesced in this and I called all my kinsmen who were in Stanley Falls and who had come in with ivory. They agreed with whatever figure I cared to name. I told the Governor that the discussion was over and he went on his way. The number of tusks coming in was staggering. With all the Belgians who came and the company I was on the best of terms; they accorded me great respect and carried out my instructions. For my part I fell in with their requirements, so that between us there was complete agreement and unanimity of purpose.

8

CARDINAL CHARLES LAVIGERIE

Speech at a Meeting of the British and Foreign Anti-Slavery Society

July 31, 1888

Cardinal Charles Lavigerie (1825–1892), the archbishop of Algiers and Carthage, was the most prominent Catholic advocate for the abolition of the slave trade in Africa in the second half of the nineteenth century. He cooperated with Leopold II in organizing the Brussels Conference of 1889–1890, which promoted international opposition to the slave trade and liquor and arms trafficking in Africa. In this speech, which Lavigerie delivered before the conference, he hails the work of David Livingstone and Britain's leadership in combating slavery under the Abolition of the Slave Trade Act of 1807 and the Abolition of Slavery Act of 1833.

"The African Slave Trade," *The Times* (London), August 1, 1888, 3.

*Lavigerie identifies Islam as the primary source of the slave trade in
Africa, and he refers specifically in this regard to "the infamous name
of Tippoo Tib [Tippu Tip]." (See Document 7.) He gives no indication
that he was aware that Tippu Tip was then an employee of the Congo
Free State. In condemning Islam, Lavigerie attempts to bridge the divide
between Catholics and the evangelical Protestants who had predominated
in the membership of the British and Foreign Anti-Slavery Society since
its establishment in 1839. Does Lavigerie articulate the same civilizing
mission found in either the speech by Livingstone (Document 1) or the
speech by Leopold II (Document 2)? Is Lavigerie's speech consistent with
the terms of the Berlin Act (Document 5)?*

I have not come among you actuated by any political thought or interest.
I am only the servant of religion, humanity, and of justice. I come here
in my capacity of veteran pastor to implore your pity for those of whom
I consider myself the father—the poor blacks of my Africa—to whose
salvation I have dedicated myself for more than 20 years, together with
my missionaries, the white fathers of Algeria. I address myself to Christian England, because nowhere can I find a greater respect for liberty
and human dignity, for it is England who in this age has taken the initiative in the abolition of slavery in the West Indies, and this she has
done with an indomitable energy and a perseverance which have at last
obtained the concurrence of all nations and the triumph of a noble
cause. *Noblesse oblige.* After having destroyed colonial slavery, England
owes it to herself to support by her sympathies those who wish to
destroy African slavery, a hundred times more horrible. She has already
taken the initiative in the persons of her numerous explorers, and particularly of her noble Livingstone. . . . She has, moreover, now in Africa
numerous and immense domains, or vast empires they may better be
called, and she cannot be uninterested in the question which is for Africa
one of life and death. Slavery in the proportions that it has now assumed
means, in effect, the approaching destruction of the black population of
the interior, with the impossibility of penetrating and civilizing the heart
of the country. I come here as a fresh witness, and, therefore, shall not
speak of what you have already heard from the recitals of your explorers. I shall only speak to you of what I know through my missionaries or
through the blacks delivered by me from slavery. My missionaries are
established in the Sahara and upon the high table-lands of Central
Africa, from the north of Nyanza to the south of Tanganyika. Eleven of
them have suffered martyrdom, while more than 50 others have died

from fatigue and hardships. Such men have the right to be heard and to be believed. Your [Lieutenant Verney Lovett] Cameron affirms with truth that half a million slaves at the least are sold every year in the interior of Africa, and I will content myself with saying that the testimony of our missionaries not only confirms, but raises this estimate for those regions where they are established. They have seen with their own eyes in the course of ten years whole provinces absolutely depopulated by the massacres of the slave-hunters, and each day they are obliged to witness scenes which point to the rapid extinction of the race. They tell me, particularly, of the province of Manyuema [Manyema], which, at the time of the death of Livingstone, was the richest in ivory and population, and which the slave-hunters have now reduced to a desert, seizing the ivory, and reducing the inhabitants to slavery in order that they may carry the ivory to the coast, after which they would be sold. The infamous name of Tippoo Tib will always be associated with this work, and it is he who has furnished Stanley with a portion of his men. The contempt for human life engendered by such examples as these, and by the passions of the slave-hunters, is so great that you can imagine nothing more horrible. . . . If this state of things continue[s], the heart of Africa will be an impenetrable desert in less than 50 years. Nevertheless, it is a wonderful country, where Europeans might live, prosper, and procure the necessaries of life. . . . The nature of the soil, the heat of the sun, and the abundance of water contribute to make this country one of the richest and most beautiful in the world. The population also was, and in some provinces still is, very numerous and happy and peaceable. It is this population which Islam is exterminating at this moment by means of her slave-hunters, and by virtue of her doctrine that the blacks are an inferior and cursed race, whom they are at liberty to treat worse than we treat our animals. For over half a century, and while our gaze was fixed upon other countries, Mahomedanism was invading, slowly and silently, with indefatigable perseverance, one half of Africa. In certain regions, those nearest us, it founded empires; the rest were secured for fomenting slavery. . . . I cannot resist saying to-day that, of the errors so fatal to Africa, the saddest is that which teaches, with Islam, that humanity is made up of two distinct races—one, that of believers, destined to command; the other, that of the cursed, as they style them, destined to serve; now, in the latter, they consider the negroes to constitute the lowest grade—viz., that on a par with cattle. . . . Having reached by their conquests the heart of a continent peopled by negroes, the Moslems have therefore betaken themselves to the work which is justified by their doctrines. By degrees, slave-trading bands, formed by them, have advanced

into the interior, coming from Morocco, from the country of the Toua-
regs, from Tunis, towards Timbuctoo [Timbuktu] and the countries which
surround the Niger; from Egypt and Zanzibar towards the region of the
lakes, and even beyond the Upper Congo, and almost to the frontiers of
the British possessions and of the Cape Colonies. Everywhere they
prosecute the same impious hunts, which feed their commerce. Sometimes the ravishers, concealing themselves along the paths, in the forests, and in the grain fields, violently carry off the negro women and
children who may pass by unattended. Things have reached such a pass
in the vicinity of the great lakes that now (I quote the words of one of
my missionaries) "every woman, every child, that strays ten minutes
away from their village has no certainty of ever returning to it." The
impunity is absolute. No negro chief of the small independent tribes,
among whom all the country is divided, has the power of repressing this
violence. While the slave-trading bands, composed of Arabs and half-
castes, and even of coast negroes, go armed to the teeth, the savage
population of the highland of Africa have no other weapons than stones,
clubs, and, at best, darts and spears. They are, therefore, incapable of
coping with the robbers who attack them and of saving themselves. . . .
The aged, the men who offer resistance, all who cannot be sold in the
markets of the interior, are killed; the women and children are seized.
All who are captured—men, women, and children—are hurried off to
some market in the interior. Then commences for them a series of
unspeakable miseries. The slaves are on foot. The men who appear the
strongest, and whose escape is to be feared, have their hands tied (and
sometimes their feet) in such fashion that walking becomes a torture to
them; and on their necks are placed yokes, which attach several of them
together. They march all day; at night, when they stop to rest, a few
handfuls of raw sorgho [sweet sorghum] are distributed among the cap-
tives. This is all their food. Next morning they must start again. But
after the first day or two the fatigue, the sufferings, and the privations
have weakened a great many. The women and the aged are the first to
halt. Then, in order to strike terror into this miserable mass of human
beings, their conductors, armed with a wooden bar to economize powder, approach those who appear to be the most exhausted and deal them
a terrible blow on the nape of the neck. The unfortunate victims utter a
cry, and fall to the ground in the convulsions of death! The terrified
troop immediately resumes its march. Terror has imbued even the
weakest with new strength. . . . In this manner the weary tramp continues—sometimes for months, when the caravan comes from a distance.
Their number diminishes daily. If, goaded by their cruel sufferings,

some attempt to rebel or to escape, their fierce masters cut them down with their swords, and leave them as they lie along the road, attached to one another by their yokes. Therefore it has been truly said that if a traveller lost the way leading from equatorial Africa to the towns where slaves are sold, he could easily find it again by the skeletons of the negroes with which it is strewed. Slavery, such as it is to-day, can in effect only be stopped by force. It is not merely by hindering the transport of slaves into Asia by means of cruisers, it is necessary to strike the evil at its root, and to destroy the markets of the interior, or to render them useless by establishing . . . barriers against slavery composed of natives led and instructed by Europeans, in order to supplement the maritime barriers formed by your cruisers. [He refers here to the British Navy's antislavery squadron.] That is what public opinion ought to obtain from civilized Governments, and what it will obtain, I am sure, if it is convinced of its utility, and does not weary in asking. But if the Governments fail to do their duty, it does not exonerate the people should they, too, fall into a fatal indifference to the fate of so many innocent victims. My friends, if this stream of blood continues to flow, take care that after so many warnings it may not be required by a just God at your hands, and those of your children. Let Christians then, band together. I speak of Christians worthy of the name, for it is necessary to have clean and honest hands for such an enterprise, and not the red hands of pirates, like those which formerly devastated America. . . . And now it is necessary to draw a practical conclusion from this discourse. What I ask from this great assembly, without distinction of persons—for however much some of us may be divided on some subjects, we are all of one accord when it becomes a matter of liberty, of humanity, of justice—is that it should, according to the individual strength of each one, join in a generous agitation in favour of a cause so grand and so pitiful. I entreat you, then, all to join me in the utterance of a loud cry, to God first of all and then to all Christian people, "God save Africa!" Yes, may God save her by exciting for her defence men animated by charity and Christian courage. Where can I better hope to have this prayer heard than in a great assembly like this, where we meet under the auspices of that admirable society which was founded, to fight against slavery and the slave trade, more than half-a-century ago, and supported by the early liberators, Thomas Clarkson, Sir Fowell Buxton, Joseph Sturge, and other noble men?

9

CHEWEMA

Statement to a British Consular Official
March 19, 1903

Chewema was a Congolese woman who fled from the Congo Free State into the British Central Africa Protectorate (BCAP), where she made this statement to a consular official. The events she recounts took place between the 1880s and approximately 1901 in the southeastern corner of the Congo Free State, in the vicinity of the Luapula River, which formed the border between the Congo Free State and the BCAP (now Malawi). Chewema's account begins when she was a girl, abducted by "Arab" (Zanzibari) slave traders from her village, and proceeds into perhaps her late teens, when she escaped to "the English side" of the river. What does this document suggest about Congolese peoples' perceptions of slave traders, the Congo Free State, and the British? What are the strengths and limitations of this document as a historical source?

My name is Chewema and I belong to the Mahusi Tribe in the Congo Free State, I remember my mother, the people in our village but have forgotten its name. I remember well that one day the Arabs made war and I together with other people were taken prisoners and were sent off to Chiwala's village at the Luapula River. When my breasts were about the size of my large toe, the Belgium soldiers with four white men called KulaKula, Chipekamansenga, Kasiera and Kachesa (these are the native names for them only). They came from Lukafu and made war with our chief Chiwala, many people were killed but the chief and his wife escaped to the English side of the Luapula, I together with other women and many tusks of ivory were captured. Part of us were sent to M'towa and Sambu and I and many others to Lukafu. The white man KulaKula was shot by Chepembera who lives at present in English Territory. When we were transported to Lukafu we were fastened together by a rope round our necks and at nighttime our hands and feet were tied

E. D. Morel Collection, Archives of the London School of Economics.

together to prevent us from escaping. At Lukafu the elder women were forced at first by the soldiers to sleep in their huts until Commandant Kasiera prohibited this. I and three other girls of my age were taken over by the Commandant to carry his water and to cultivate his gardens. After one month at Lukafu, I and the three other girls were sent to M'pwetu, we were tied together the whole way but on our arrival at M'pwetu the white men there took off the ropes. I was taken by the white man called Lutina as his wife's servant. None of the women at M'pwetu were allowed to leave the station, many however managed to escape to the English side, also some soldiers were allowed to take their women with them when leaving the station but others had to remain whether they had children by them or not.

At M'pwetu I witnessed the killing of two natives who had stolen rubber from the Government Stores. By the order of the white man call[ed] Lutina the two natives were beaten by his soldiers with a hippo hide whip, after this they were made to stand up, the soldiers then threw bricks on them till they died. One native was from Chewerchewera's village very near M'pwetu and was buried by his relations, the other who had no relations so near was thrown into the Lake Mweru.

I have been two rainy seasons at M'pwetu till I had the opportunity to go with another woman to the English side, also I have been there two rainy seasons, from there I went to Lake Nyasa where I arrived last month.

The above statement was made before me and the followi[n]g witnesses on the nineteenth day of March 1903, and interpreted by the two natives Bwana Timothy and Alexander Ned.

Witnesses: James B. Yule
T. B. H. Piers
C. T. Candy

10

JOHN AND JOHAN

Statement to a British Consular Official
March 19, 1903

John and Johan were African subjects of the British Central Africa Protectorate (BCAP) who served as soldiers in the neighboring Congo Free State around 1899–1900. The events in this statement occurred in the vicinity of Lake Tanganyika, on the state's eastern border. In describing the conflicts between African soldiers and Belgian officers, the men are probably referring to the aftermath of a major revolt by the force publique *at Ndirfi in 1897. The men made this statement to a British consular official in the BCAP after their return home. What does this document convey about the tactics and strength of the* force publique? *What does it convey about the power of the Congo Free State?*

We John and Johan, natives of Karonga, Lake Nyasa, British Central Africa, do hereby declare that about four years ago we were engaged by Mr. Mohun to serve him as soldiers for the period of three years during his constructing of a telegraph line in the Congo Free State.

On our arrival in the Congo Free State we learnt from the inhabitants and the government soldiers that there is always war between the white men, the soldiers and the natives.

The reason of a war and the constant troubles are as follows: —

Long ago the Belgium Officials hanged the soldiers for their bad behaviour. They hanged so many that this created a vengence to such an extent that all soldiers formed a ring under the headman, at that time the sergeant called Yankoffu; with the object to kill all officers at the different stations on and near the Lake Tanganyika. This they did and took all the guns and ammunition. They then formed a stockade and made Yankoffu their chief. Later on they were attacked by a strong force of the Belgiums, also we under Mr. Mohun attacked them, we killed many people but could not get Yankoffu. Most of his people crossed the Lake to German Territory taking with them the captured guns and ammunition. After this other Belgium officers re-occupied the plundered sta-

---

E. D. Morel Collection, Archives of the London School of Economics.

tions but from that time the officers became afraid of the soldiers. When we were there one officer of Marabo station about ten days from Lake Tanganyika, thrashed a soldier with a hippo hide whip. Sometime later the same officer received from the same soldier a letter and when reading the same the latter shot him dead. We two, and many other soldiers were given orders to catch the murderer, we went after him for many days but could not find him. The white men are so afraid of the soldiers that they let them do whatever they like, they rape, murder and steal everything of the inhabitants, and if the chief or villagers object they are often shot dead on the spot. The officers all know this but they never take any notice of it as they are afraid to punish their soldiers. Another officer called by the natives Kaputimasinga died long ago at his station Rivarenga on the Lake shore of Tanganyika. At this station he punished the natives by cutting off their hands, ears, etc. etc., or hanged them according to the crime.

The above statement was made before me and the following witnesses on the nineteenth day of March 1903 and interpreted by the two natives Bwana Timothy and Alexander Ned.

Witnesses: James B. Yule
T. B. H. Piers
C. T. Candy

11

ANTOINE BOONGO

Oral History regarding the Arrival of European Officers and Missionaries at Wangata in the Equateur District

ca. 1883–1896

This is one of many oral histories collected by the Catholic missionary Father Edmond Boelaert in 1953–1954 in an effort to record Congolese perspectives on the arrival of "whites" (Europeans) in the central basin.

Annales Aequatoria 16 (1995): 36–38. Translated from French by Martine Guyot-Bender.

Boongo was, as a boy, the servant of Charles Lemaire, the first commissioner of the Equateur District, between November 1890 and June 1893. This account spans the period from 1883 to 1896 and focuses on the vicinity of Coquilhatville (now Mbandaka), the capital of the Equateur District, at the confluence of the Congo and Ruki rivers. Boongo recounts the arrival of a series of Europeans, who were initially thought to be wandering spirits of dead ancestors. The Europeans proceeded to establish trading stations and government posts. It is noteworthy that Boongo does not refer to treaties (see Document 3), nor does he indicate whether the Europeans were company agents or government officials. Most of the Europeans are identified in the selection by their nicknames; their actual names, if known, are given in the footnotes. The meanings of nicknames could be significant, as in the case of Lemaire, known as Ikoka, meaning "he who shoots people." "Mr. Banks" (Charles Banks) is the only European identified by his proper name. Banks, an Englishman, was a member of the American Baptist Missionary Union and played a critical role in advocating for the Congolese peoples in the district. According to Boongo, Banks could end a war in Congo with a letter to Europe. What were the most important ways in which Congolese peoples distinguished between one European and another? How should you, as a historian, account for the fact that this oral history was recorded by a Catholic missionary sixty years after the events occurred?

The first whites who arrived here were Wefa and Bantsetse.[1] They landed at Wangata, where the SAB [*Société Anonyme Belge pour le Commerce du Haut-Congo*] factory is located.[2] The Wangata chased them off;

[1] Wefa was Louis Putzeys, who worked for the Anonymous Belgian Company for Trade in Upper-Congo (Société Anonyme Belge pour le Commerce du Haut-Congo). Bantsetse was Lieutenant Alphonse Vangele, who was appointed by Henry Stanley to head the station of the International Association of the Congo established in 1883 near Wangata (referred to in this text as the Equateur station). This station, approximately seven hundred miles from the coast, was known as Equateur or Equateurville. In 1886 it was renamed Coquilhatville and designated as the capitol of the Equateur District. It is now named Mbandaka and is the capitol of the Equateur Province of the Democratic Republic of Congo. This information is from the name index on the *Centre Aequatoria* website, www.aequatoria.be/04frans/030themes/0331blegende_abbr.htm (hereafter cited as *Aequatoria* name index), accessed August 15, 2013; David Lagergren, *Mission and State in the Congo, 1885–1903* (Lund, Sweden: Gleerup, 1970), 53, 58–60.

[2] It is not clear when exactly this factory, or station, was established. The SAB itself was established in 1892. Boongo is recalling here the arrival of the first whites some time before the station existed. As the previous footnote indicates, he appears to be referring to the whites who established the station for the International Association of the Congo

they did not want them, because they thought that they were wandering spirits of the dead. After being chased off, the whites settled on an island called Bonkoso.

There, beyond the river, a man called Eluwa, from up river, a slave of the patriarch Ikenge, met them as he was returning from getting palm wine in Ntsambala. They gave him two vessels, one with beads, the other [with] cowrie shells, as well as two pieces of *bafulunkoi* fabric.[3] They accompanied him.

His master told him: "You are stupid. These spirits, I chased them off, and you, you bring them back here?" Ikenge became angry, but the other patriarchs calmed him, saying: "No, leave them alone. We will see." The strangers took out a meter stick and they were given a small piece of land, where the SAB is. We did not give it to them for free; they paid five vessels of cowries and beads, and six pieces of *ifulunkoi* fabric.

Then they dismantled their tents, they built a house . . . and they raised a fence. When they had finished the fence, chickens from local residents entered; they killed them and ate them. These chickens belonged to Ikenge's mother, Mbela.

The first whites left and others came to replace them. Two whites came to succeed Stanley: Mpumu Mbembo and Katamadala.[4] When Ikenge's mother asked them about the chickens, they hit her with a stick on the bridge of her nose and she died.

The Wangata beat the war tom-toms [drums]. We fought because they had killed Ikenge's mother. The Wangata killed a Hausa soldier. However, they killed no one else. But other people in the area of Bolenge killed Matayembu.[5]

Ikoka and another white, his adjunct, came to replace them.[6] Ikoka did not want anyone to pass in a canoe. If someone happened to pass by, he called him; if [the person] did not want to come, he killed him with his gun.

---

near Wangata in 1883. In the text that follows, he probably recounts a number of events out of chronological order, but within an accurate time frame of several years.

[3]Beads, cowrie shells, and fabric were forms of currency.

[4]Stanley left Congo in 1884. The identity of Mpumu Mbembo is unknown. Katamandala was Guillaume Casman (1854–1885), who succeeded Vangele as head of the Equateur station in December 1884 (*Aequatoria* name index; Lagergren, *Mission and State in the Congo*, 63).

[5]The identity of Matayembu is unknown.

[6]Ikoka was Charles Lemaire (1863–1925), the first commissioner of the Equateur District. He took up this post at Coquilhatville in November or December 1890 (Lagergren, *Mission and State in the Congo*, 98). Ikoka means "he who shoots people" (Osumaka Likaka, *Naming Colonialism: History and Collective Memory in the Congo, 1870–1960* [Madison: University of Wisconsin Press, 2009], 165).

One day, as some Boloki people were coming back from a trading voyage downstream, he called them, but they did not want to come. A sentry shot his gun. Then he [set off in another boat].[7] At this time, I was a small boy.[8] But he did not catch up with the Boloki, who had escaped.

Upon his return, Ikoka saw the land of Mbandaka.[9] We stayed there, at the SAB [station at Equateur], for one week, then we went back [to Mbandaka] to begin the post of Coquilhatville. They built two houses. When people came he said to them: "Be aware that a white, a military man, will be coming."

After one month, Mr. Tembeleke arrived.[10] He was a military man. When Tembeleke arrived, Ikoka left, abandoning the houses. Mr. Tembeleke settled there. He left the SAB post and moved it to Irebu. The Wangata gathered the canoes and traveled to Irebu.[11]

Then he called the village chiefs. They came. He said to them: "I called you about the rubber." One week later, he called them again and said to them: "Now, I give you a sentry with a gun in each village." He gave this order to the sentries: "If they do not want to produce rubber, you must bring me the hands of the people you killed." In the village that did not bring a basket of rubber, they killed two people, maybe three.[12]

Because of these deaths, there was a last battle with Mbandaka [Wajiko] from up river.[13] So many people were killed that blood was one meter high; it came up to the thighs. One native of Mbandaka, a servant of Mr. Banks, escaped, saying: "The white of the state has created chaos in the land."[14] Mr. Banks, the Protestant missionary, took his horse and set off for Mbandaka. When he arrived he saw blood flowing like a river. He stopped in the hamlet of Bofeke l'Asimba, and said: "The white of the state has created chaos in the land. He has killed everyone. I am

[7]It is not clear if "he" refers to the sentry or Lemaire.

[8]Boongo probably mentions his age because he was Lemaire's servant at this time.

[9]It is unclear where Lemaire was returning from. Mbandaka appears to refer here to both a land and its people.

[10]Tembeleke was Léon Fiévez, who succeeded Lemaire as district commissioner in June 1893. He remained in this position until 1896.

[11]Irebu is located downriver, at the confluence of Lake Tumba and the Congo River.

[12]These events probably occurred in 1894 (Lagergren, *Mission and State in the Congo*, 125).

[13]Boongo refers here not to Mbandaka (Coquilhatville), where events such as the following never occurred, but to the land and people of Mbandaka, and specifically Mbandaka Wajiko, located south of Coquilhatville. Hence, the battle was started upriver. State forces conducted a massacre in this village in October 1896 in reprisal for a short-fall in rubber. The horrific aftermath was witnessed by the missionary Charles Banks (Lagergren, *Mission and State in the Congo*, 175–78).

[14]Banks was posted at the American Baptist Missionary Union's station at Bolenge, just south of the massacre.

going to send a letter to Europe, to the King." After he sent the letter to Europe, the war ended.[15]

. . . The people were furious with the Wangata, because they had welcomed the spirits. They called death upon them for this.

[15]Soon after the massacre, Coquilhatville was visited by Governor-General Théophile Wahis, who toured Congo for ten months in 1896–1897. Wahis met with Banks and was eventually persuaded that the massacre at Mbandaka Wajiko had occurred. He dismissed the responsible officer from his post, forbade punitive expeditions, and ordered that African sentries should no longer be posted unsupervised in villages. Wahis's reforms had a lasting, relatively positive effect on the conditions of the Congolese peoples in the vicinity of Coquilhatville (Lagergren, *Mission and State in the Congo*, 175–78). It is noteworthy that in a previous confrontation with a state official in late 1895, Banks had threatened to take his criticisms to Europe (ibid., 130–37). These separate events might be conflated in this account.

12

BALOFO IS'A MBOYO AND EKOMBE IS'EK'OMBOLA

Oral History regarding the Arrival of Whites at Ikau in the Equateur District

ca. 1889–1896

*This is another of the many oral histories collected by the Catholic missionary Father Edmond Boelaert (see Document 11). This history was recorded and then conveyed to Boelaert by two Congolese intermediaries, Bernard Boyau and Augustin Ekumbo. It addresses the period from approximately 1889 to 1896 in the territories of the Anglo-Belgian India Rubber and Exploration Company (ABIR) and the Anonymous Belgian Company for Trade in Upper-Congo (*Société Anonyme Belge pour le Commerce du Haut-Congo, *or SAB) in the Equateur District. The events occurred between Basankusu and Bongandanga on the Lopori River. The account describes how company agents and government officials initially induced the Congolese to collect rubber and later enforced their increasing demands with the violence of sentries and soldiers, despite the protests of missionaries. The ensuing "rubber war" was settled by Waisi, Governor-General Théophile Wahis (1844–1921), who toured the district in July*

Annales Aequatoria 17 (1996): 306–8. Translated from French by Martine Guyot-Bender.

*and August 1896. (Wahis's own account of events in Congo appears in
Document 17.) What does this document suggest about the ways in which
Congolese perceptions of Europeans changed over time? What does it
suggest about the administrative organization and authority of the Congo
Free State?*

Formerly, we did not know of whites in our land. . . . The first whites
we ever saw were Protestant missionaries. We were in Benkuka-Sekea,
near Linlangi. That is where we lived. The Protestant missionaries came
aboard their canoes, which were like boats.[1] We marveled at the whites'
canoes. The Protestants settled first in Basankoso [Basankusu], specifically at Ikau.[2]

. . . After the Protestants, more whites arrived. But they did not come
all the way to our region. They remained on the Lulonga [River].[3] Their
names were: Wilima, who felt free to do whatever he liked; after him,
there came a white of the [Congo Free State].[4] Then, two companies
settled in Basankoso.[5] We did not know their names, and the elders
did not care to know. Those two whites were called Bomende and Bon-

[1]The author is probably comparing the missionaries' "canoes" to boats of the 1950s.
The first boats in which the missionaries arrived resembled in their dimensions long,
shallow-draft dugouts (*pirogues*) in which Congolese peoples traveled. Members of the
Congo Balolo Mission first arrived in the region in August 1889 aboard the *Henry Reed*,
a seventy-one-foot, shallow-draft vessel covered with a fabric canopy on poles. Though
this vessel was relatively long for a *pirogue*, it would not have been unfamiliar to the
Congolese, as it was comparable to the large canoes in which slaves were transported
through Basankusu. It was also, however, a side-wheel paddle steamer with a small
wood-burning engine at its center, which probably prompted the authors to liken the
pirogues to boats (*bateaux*).
[2]Basankusu is located at the juncture of the Lopori and Maringa rivers. The Congo
Balolo Mission established a station at Ikau in 1889 (David Lagergren, *Mission and State
in the Congo, 1885–1903* [Lund, Sweden: Gleerup, 1970], 91).
[3]The Lopori and Maringa rivers flow into the Lulonga River.
[4]Wilima was Gustave-Émile Sarrazyn (1864–1915). At this time he was a senior officer
of the *force publique*. Between 1896 and 1898, he was the commissioner of the Equateur
District. According to the British consular official Roger Casement, Sarrazyn's nickname (which Casement rendered as "Widjima") meant "Darkness." (See Document 22.)
This information is from the name index on the *Centre Aequatoria* website, http://www
.aequatoria.be/04frans/030themes/0331blegende_abbr.htm (hereafter cited as *Aequatoria* name index), accessed August 15, 2013; Lagergren, *Mission and State in the Congo*,
237.
[5]The Anglo-Belgian India Rubber and Exploration Company (ABIR) and the Anonymous Belgian Company for Trade in Upper-Congo (Société Anonyme Belge pour le Commerce du Haut-Congo, or SAB) were both founded in 1892 and began to expand into the
Equateur District after 1893. ABIR exploited the basin between the Lopori and Maringa
rivers, and the SAB exploited the areas north and south of the rivers.

jolongo.[6] Very annoying whites. But two elders, Wane and Engbanjala, accompanied them for a visit to the Protestants. Upon returning, the two elders took counsel and wondered: "Those whites are very annoying, how are we going to get rid of them?" They then looked for ways to kill them.

Soon after, [the elders] see a kite [a bird] and say: "White, see a bird; shoot it for us with your gun." Checking his pockets, the white did not find his pistol. . . . When the two elders noticed that the white did not have a gun, they killed Bomende and Bonjolongo because of their abuses.[7]

After hearing about the murder of the two whites, the Protestants sent a letter to Wilima, the white of the government.[8] He was a bad white. And thus began a war that resulted in the depopulation. But when the Protestants realized that the blacks were decimated, they asked the state to stop the war.

In the meantime, a white called Ilombo, and his younger brother called Moto, came and created an administrative station.[9] In Boyeka, there was a company called Molo.[10] Its concessions were in Bonginda, Losombo, Bobanga, Wenga, and Lokoloko-Ifomi. Another company was in Bokakata.[11] Its head was called Ekot'Olongo, a white of the SAB [*Société Anonyme Belge*].[12] The white chose the most influential people to buy him whatever he wanted. The white gave them *mitako* [currency of brass rods or copper wire] to buy him ivory tusks, and rubber. The white called Ilombo ordered: "Bring me the rubber so that I can buy it." And the

[6]Bomende was César Peters, lieutenant to Bonjolongo, Lucien Termolle (1860–1893), a commissaire first class of the state. He was assigned to the state post at Basankusu in 1891 (*Aequatoria* name index; Lagergren, *Mission and State in the Congo*, 100–101). Here the original text conflates the two companies and these two men. It is noteworthy that the men were officers assigned to a state post, and not company employees. The confusion in this account reflects the difficulty that Congolese peoples faced in distinguishing between state officers and company employees due to ill-defined authority over administration and law enforcement.

[7]The men were ambushed and killed by Congolese near Basankusu on January 16, 1893 (Lagergren, *Mission and State in the Congo*, 100–101).

[8]The letter was probably sent by J. R. Ellery of the Congo Balolo Mission, who had buried the two bodies. The district commissioner at this time was Charles Lemaire. Note that Is'a Mboyo refers here to "Wilima" [see note 4], indicating his confusion about which European occupied which position at this time. As we saw in Document 11, Lemaire's nickname was Ikoka (Lagergren, *Mission and State in the Congo*, 98, 105).

[9]Ilombo was a company official. Moto's identity is unknown (*Aequatoria* name index). It appears that in this narrative, Bomende and Bonjolongo, and Ilombo and Moto, have been mistakenly switched as state officers and company employees.

[10]This probably refers to ABIR.

[11]This refers to the SAB.

[12]Ekot'Olongo's identity is unknown.

blacks responded: "What is rubber?" ["]Isn't it true that you do not eat the fruit of a reddish plant?["] [Ilombo asked.][13] ["]Well, cut off the vines of these plants, coat the latex [white fluid] on your belly, then remove the rubber."[14] The elders came home at harvest time and brought the rubber to the white. He bought it with brass. And the white left.

One day he said to the blacks: "Take banana leaves or gourds, and go again to collect rubber. Collect the latex that comes out of the vines. Back in the village, add the liquid from the Costus bokàakò [a plant] and you will see what happens."[15] The elders did what the white had ordered, and saw that the latex formed one single ball. They took all the balls and gave them to the white. The white bought them with beads, brass and clothing.

Having seen the rubber, the white rejoiced intensely. He says to himself: "What was lost has been found, the search is over" (quoting from the Mongo proverb *Itswàki yôlenya lokoso lôsìla*). Then he ordered: "Go back for seven days to collect rubber, each one of you bring me a basket of rubber." The blacks followed his orders, but when they came back, all those who had not filled up their baskets were shot. At the marketplace the white had posted a soldier in charge of killing those who did not fill up their baskets. The blacks were frightened and realized that at first the white had lured them. They then refused to collect rubber because of those killings. But the whites did not stop demanding more rubber. They had given guns to their soldiers and sent them to all the villages in search of rubber. The whites had many blacks killed.

Then, a white of the state nicknamed Is'Ongembe arrived, accompanied by captain Asito, a white from Jamani who had killed many people.[16] That is why today we talk about the "Jamani war" in memory of this white during the rubber war.

At this time, a white Protestant missionary, nicknamed Jefeli, was in Bongandanga.[17] He arrived at Ikau and declared: "Why are these people so exterminated here in Congo? I am going to Europe to put the question to the main chief Lowa Yapolu [King Leopold II of Belgium].

---

[13]Rubber was gathered from the landolphia plant, which bears fruit.

[14]The latex thickened on the skin and could then be peeled off as "rubber."

[15]"Costus bokàakò" is a member of the Costaceae family. This was probably *Costus phyllocephalus*, a plant used by the Congolese for food and medicinal purposes.

[16]Is'Ongembe was Bror Hagström (1871–1912), an officer of the *force publique*. Asito's identity is unknown (*Aequatoria* name index).

[17]Jefeli was probably A. E. Ruskin, a member of the Congo Balolo Mission stationed at Bongandanga after 1895 (Lagergren, *Mission and State in the Congo*, 172).

I am going to tell him that the Congo is being exterminated, maybe he will have the war stopped." Then he went away very angry.

Then, the king sent a governor named Waisi [Governor-General Wahis] to stop and ban the war.[18] He found the white of the state Is'Ongembe and exclaimed to him: "How come the people in Congo are exterminated in such a way? Leave, and go to the Ntomba, you have killed many people."[19] Waisi banned the war, and that was the end of the rubber.

[18]Wahis corresponded with Ruskin at this time (ibid., 172–73).

[19]The Ntomba were located elsewhere on the Lopori River. This was probably a demotion.

13

BRUNO HAFALA

Oral History regarding Events on the Maringa River in the Equateur District

ca. 1899–1901

This is another of the many oral histories collected by the Catholic missionary Father Edmond Boelaert (see Documents 11 and 12). It addresses the period from approximately 1899 to 1901 in the territory of the Anglo-Belgian India Rubber and Exploration Company (ABIR) in the Equateur District. The events occurred in a region to the east of Basankusu and to the west of Baringa, on the Maringa River. It sheds light on conditions under ABIR during the rubber boom. The Lifumba people initially fought ABIR, and then retreated eastward, only to be attacked by the Bakela people. The Lifumba then returned west to submit to ABIR's rule. This account is particularly interesting because it includes the arrest of a company agent by a state official. Did the Lifumba people act consistently or inconsistently in their sometimes peaceful, sometimes violent relations with the whites? Did the whites act consistently or inconsistently? How can you explain their actions in these terms?

Annales Aequatoria 17 (1996): 274–76. Translated from French by Martine Guyot-Bender.

The war started when a sentry came from the post of Bokongoonlo. He was called Lokwama. He ordered us to collect rubber. The next day, the white himself arrived. He was a white from the ABIR company. He said to the villagers: "Give me a name." And we named him Bosekota.[1] He gave us a ten-day deadline to start harvesting rubber. After the deadline, we started to harvest, but he killed two persons: Is'a Logonfr, who was from Baenga, and MpEtsi, who was from Lifumba. Their executioner was Lokwama. We crossed the river and settled in Baringa [on the Maringa River] especially in Boilinga. The beach was in Ingonda.[2] Lokamba, the white of the ABIR company, was posted to our location.[3] After him, there were successively: Ilomba and Is'e'wanga.[4] While we were weighing the rubber, we were fighting: they with guns, we with arrows. The guns in question were pistols and Albini [rifles]. They paid us with harpoons [fishing spears?], shoes, bedsheets, indigo fabrics and *ceintures rouges* [red cotton cloths wrapped around the waist by African soldiers of the state].

Then the white called MpEtsi arrived and ordered us to [collect] the rubber.[5] He paid us with knives, long machetes, salt and cowrie shells. While we traded in that fashion, sentries killed people. Because of that we disarmed the sentries. It is possible that the Protestant missionaries were in the vicinity. But only Jimisi and Elese made it all the way to our location with their preaching.[6]

The white who arrived at our homeland was Longwango of the ABIR.[7] He had seen our blacksmith Elumbu as he was working hard at his trade.

---

[1] Bosekota was Albert Vander Cruysen, who departed for Congo in 1899 and headed stations in the Equateur District in 1903 and 1904. This information is from the name index on the *Centre Aequatoria* website, http://www.aequatoria.be/04frans/030themes/0331ble gende_abbr.htm (hereafter cited as *Aequatoria* name index), accessed August 15, 2013.

[2] The meaning of "beach" is unclear. It might refer to the shore where goods were loaded and unloaded from canoes.

[3] The identity of Lokamba is unknown.

[4] Ilomba was Mr. Angrey, and Is'e'wanga was Lieutenant Ernest Remont (1872–1901), a state agent (*Aequatoria* name index).

[5] MpEtsi was H. Tegner, who was stationed at Basankusu in 1896–1900 (*Aequatoria* name index).

[6] The identities of Jimisi and Elese are unknown. They were probably missionaries from the nearest mission station, the Congo Balolo Mission at Baringa, which was later a source of intense criticism of the state.

[7] Longwango was Lieutenant Knud Jespersen (1873–1941), a state official. Jespersen began his service in Congo in 1898 at Bala Londji on the Momboyo River in the Equateur District, outside the ABIR and the Société Anonyme Belge pour le Commerce du Haut-Congo (SAB) concessions. Over the next three years, he traveled through these companies' territories (*Aequatoria* name index; David Lagergren, *Mission and State in the Congo, 1885–1903* [Lund, Sweden: Gleerup, 1907], 128).

He ordered his sentry to kill him, and he was killed. A white missionary told him: "You acted badly." The missionary sent a report downstream. He was called Ngenangena.[8] The soldier who killed Elumbu was Jangi. The other soldiers were Lonkonjo, Likyo and Wunju. They returned downstream. No one ever came back.

Arrival of the White of the State

While we were gathering rubber, a white of the state, called Basikotsi, arrived at the post and looked for the white of the ABIR.[9] He had him arrested; he was handcuffed and taken downstream. And the white [of the state] said: "It is over with the ABIR. The state is taking back its full authority." He found us in Baringa, at the beach at Ingonda. Another white called Is'e'Ongembe arrived.[10] Then he went back to Basankoso [Basankusu]. After that, the Bakela invaded us. Dressed in beast hides, armed with spears and shields, they went from house to house beating and dispersing us. We, the Lifumba, got scared and, here we are today, settled in the vicinity of Basankoso.

We are in Basankoso because of the abuses of the ABIR company and because of you Belgians. At that time there was not yet money or taxes. We were still at the entry of our new location when Itoko the white from the state ordered us to collect rubber again to give to the white called Longwango, who declared: "We do not want it, return to Baringa."[11] And we responded to him, "We did not accept this." We went all the way to Basankoso to complain to the administrator Is'e'Ongembe. We were five men: Bofondo, Linlinga, Lokembya, Lomboto and Etoi. After listening to us, he told us to live in the south of Waka and to send him rubber from there.[12] Is'e'Ongembe was the main administrator. We worked without compensation. Money was introduced with the [harvesting of] copal and palm kernels. This is why a part of the Lifumba came here while another one stayed in Befale. The white then ordered [us] to pay the tax. We paid the tax at Kukulu, then the whites became more numerous. Silence.

---

[8]The identity of Ngenangena is unknown.

[9]The identity of Basikotsi is unknown. The name means "the whips" (*Aequatoria* name index).

[10]Is'e'Ongembe was Bror Hagström (1871–1912), an officer of the *force publique* (*Aequatoria* name index).

[11]Itoko was Mr. Milan (*Aequatoria* name index).

[12]Waka was located upstream of Basankusu on the Maringa River.

14

NICOLAS AFOLEMBE

Oral History regarding Conditions in the Equateur District

ca. 1885–1908

This is another of the many oral histories collected by the Catholic missionary Father Edmond Boelaert (see Documents 11–13). Afolembe's account covers the life span of the Congo Free State, from approximately 1885 to 1908. He initially recalls life under the rule of the "Arabs" (Zanzibaris) near the headwaters of the Lopori River. He then recounts events in the same area after it became the easternmost territory of the Anglo-Belgian India Rubber and Exploration Company (ABIR). This account illuminates years of terrible violence and a remarkable instance of cooperation between Congolese peoples in resisting ABIR. Afolembe also observes improvements as the governance of the territory was transferred from ABIR to the Congo Free State in 1906 and then to the Belgian government in 1908. What are the similarities and differences between this oral history and the ones in Documents 11–13?

[1.] Arabs

In our region, and specifically in the chiefdom of Losaila, it is true that Arabs arrived.[1] One of their chiefs called Simba [lion] lived in a village called Liotsi. This is where our mission Simba is now located. Normally, this mission should be called "Mission Liotsi." But our elders, since the departure of the Arabs from our homeland, did not forget the place where their chief resided. And when the whites arrived, they still lived on the same site. And they called this station "Simba." And because all Losaila was under the rule of this Arab chief, until now we are called "Losaila-Simba."

---

[1]Under the leadership of the Zanzibari Tippu Tip, Manyema slave traders moved into the eastern half of the Lopori-Maringa basin after 1885 and gained control of it by 1892. Simba is located near the headwaters of the Lopori River.

Annales Aequatoria 17 (1996): 291–95. Translated from French by Martine Guyot-Bender.

At the time of the Arabs (Batambatamba in our Longando language), a man was [treated] like a wild beast. Our own people had to do likewise. In the same fashion, they killed people without pity and established harems. Personally, I know two: one who recently died, and another who is currently our chief. A very old man. . . .

[2.] The Harvest of the Rubber

After the departure of the Arabs from us, the Bongando, they were replaced by the rubber whites.[2] The elders call that time "the period of the ABIR Company."[3] Their posts were Yahuma, Simba, Bolese and Betutu. The whites who were in these stations, we do not know their real names. But the villagers gave them names, nicknames. Such as: Longange, Itomotom'a Likoso, Lilang'atumbe, Likoke, Bokunjw'a Lomuma, BongEnge Bolembo, Nkoy'Isenge, Bambelu and many others.[4] Their work was to impose rubber on the natives.

The rubber was not purchased at [just] any time or any place. There were precise days and places. It was bought only at the places I already mentioned: Yahuma, Simba, Betutu and Bolese. (Here I do not speak about the Bongando region on the other side of the Lopori [River], but our side of the Lopori.)

At the time of weighing, if your rubber was lower than the required weight, they whip you and throw you in jail.

Each village had a *capita* [sentry] appointed by the whites to make the people harvest the rubber.[5] This is the way the people suffered. How were those *capitas* treated? And why? At each weighing of rubber, if the weight of the rubber for a *capita* or someone in his group was insufficient, the *capita* is punished, and the punishment of the population is the *chicotte* [whip] and the jail. Before going to the weighing, they checked

---

[2] It took the Congo Free State approximately a decade, from the late 1880s to 1898, to drive the Zanzibari slave traders out of the eastern basin. Toward this end, the state established a post at Basankusu in 1890 (Robert Harms, "The World Abir Made: The Maringa-Lopori Basin, 1885–1903," *African Economic History* 12 [1983]: 126).

[3] ABIR was founded in 1892, and it established a post at Basankusu in 1893 (ibid., 128).

[4] Longange was Mr. Van Cauter. The identities of Itomotom'a Likoso and Lilang' atumbe are unknown. The name Lilang'atumbe means "burner of fields." The identities of Likoke, Bokunjw'a Lomuma, BongEnge Bolembo, Nkoy'Isenge, and Bambelu are unknown. This information is from the name index on the *Centre Aequatoria* website, http://www.aequatoria.be/04frans/030themes/0331blegende_abbr.htm (hereafter cited as *Aequatoria* name index), accessed August 15, 2013.

[5] The term *capita* was borrowed from the Portuguese. It designated an African employed by the Portuguese as an intermediary or representative in trade, especially the slave trade.

that the weight of the harvest of each was sufficient. The one who harvested the least was killed. Thus many people died.

I have already mentioned the four posts where they bought rubber: Yahuma, Simba, Betutu and Bolese. I will speak now about the events that happened in Betutu.[6] Then I will tell what happened in Simba.

They weighed the rubber in Betutu, that is to say in the chiefdoms of Bokote and Nkok's Lopori. These two chiefdoms constituted a single chiefdom.

Having found that the suffering has overwhelmed [them] and that rubber has become rare, they ran away. They crossed the Lopori upstream, distancing themselves from their own territory to settle in Mompono on the Luwo River.[7] They stayed there some time. One day, the Mompono killed Boalangi's son. Due to this, they become upset and declare: "It is better that we go back to our homeland, even if they killed us, it does not matter." And they went back.

Many feared the suffering that they had endured earlier. That is why they started to settle along the way, creating new sites. A father and his children, and so on. Another group of people crossed the Lopori and went back to their former villages.

Those who stayed along the way created large chiefdoms: Maringa, Nsema, Balanga and Nkok's Lopori. Hearing that some people had returned to their former territory (chiefdom Bokote), the whites returned to Betutu station and reinstated the harvesting of rubber. The white who was the chief at the time was Longange. His replacement was Lilang'atumbe.

Still, and as I said earlier, if the rubber was not sufficient, one is punished. Now the rubber has become rare and the villagers had no other way to harvest rubber.[8] How did they manage?

. . . Those who had crossed the Lopori and those who had settled along the way during their exodus from Mompono took counsel and decided to set fire to all the stations where whites resided, starting with Betutu. They gathered for war. One day, they attacked the white and his men, and they won the fight. They forced the white to leave. The residents of Betutu boarded him entirely naked on a canoe only protected by some wild leaves, and he was taken to Simba.

---

[6] Betutu station was probably located upstream of Simba.

[7] The Luwo River is probably a tributary of the Maringa River, near its headwaters. In 1910, there was a settlement called Mompono, located near the confluence of the Maringa River and a small tributary. A significant population of the Luwo (Luo) people lived in the eastern Congo.

[8] The shortage of wild rubber vines throughout ABIR's territory became acute in 1903–1904.

[3.] In Simba

Rubber was weighed at Simba, in the chiefdom of Losaila-Simba. The white who was the chief at the time was BolEmbo, along with other whites.[9]

When the villagers saw that Betutu station had been destroyed, they planned a greater attack that would burn the Simba station. With the population of Losaila-Simba, they took counsel and had the same idea; then they assembled for war.

Seeing this, the whites in Simba erected a lattice fence and posted guards on each side. That way they would be warned of an attack, and could enclose the servants and soldiers within the fence, which would be immediately locked.

One morning, the war tom-toms [drums], trumpets, and songs of war were heard. A large group of men arrived and hid. At that moment, the whites, the soldiers and the staff went into the enclosure. The white in charge distributed ammunition to the soldiers, with the following instructions: "Do not shoot before they get closer; also do not shoot one after the other. Shoot all together on my command, and only if they attack us first with their arrows." Some time later, the villagers approached with the sound of tom-toms and trumpets, and war songs. Making a lot of noise, they stopped a few meters away, holding their shields. They [had] covered their bodies in white kaolin and charcoal. They resemble leopards.

Soon afterward, they fire arrows toward the whites and their soldiers. Then the white orders the soldiers to shoot. After the first firing, you see dead bodies covering the other side of the fence in the way ants die when one sets them on fire. After the second firing, you cannot see anyone left standing; all had fled and many were dead. Those who fled looted the whites' belongings on their way. All were scattered. Those who were behind the fence came out and chased them. Those who were caught were killed to extinguish their wickedness.

After having annihilated the natives, the whites forbade soldiers to kill people. They ordered them to catch them and put them in jail. This war between the whites and the villagers did not end soon. Often, villagers fought against soldiers, stole their guns and killed them.

Subsequently, the whites sent a message to Basankusu, and many soldiers from Basankusu [came], along with more whites. Those whites were called Mbulamatale.[10] The soldiers fought the villagers and annihilated them.

---

[9]The identity of BolEmbo is unknown.
[10]The identity of these whites is unknown.

Realizing that they would not win, the villagers gathered their courage and designated the most courageous one among them to be the intermediary between them and the whites. The intermediary went to tell the whites what the villagers wanted, that is to say peace. Then they gave back the guns they had stolen from soldiers, as a sign of the return of peace and the end of all palavers [negotiations and disputes].

The whites agreed and the people approached the whites again. We began to execute their corvées and peacefulness returned to our country.

From then on, they began to design roads for the villages. Roads were built between villages. Interclan wars had stopped. People were beginning to be paid in brass. The country became organized as it should be so that all would be as it is now.[11]

Since that time when villagers and whites of the state had signed a peace accord, until now, we call that time "Belesi," that is to say, Belgium. That is why, in our region, and until now, if someone acts like a villager, he is told: "You, you act like a brute; you don't know that Belesi has come?"

[11]This probably refers to reforms following the transfer of administrative authority over the territory from ABIR to the Congo Free State in September 1906.

15

THE REVEREND JOHN MURPHY

Testimony

November 18, 1895

The Reverend John Murphy was an Irish member of the American Baptist Missionary Union who had already worked for nine years in Congo when he provided this information about conditions there. Humanitarians subsequently treated this as the first public indictment of the Congo Free State in Europe by a reliable eyewitness. Murphy largely addresses the same period and the same region, the Equateur District, covered by the Congolese oral

"The Congo Free State," *The Times* (London), November 18, 1895.

histories found in Documents 11–14. Murphy acknowledges that he previously complained to the state about its abuse of Congolese peoples in 1888, 1889, and 1894. What reasons might he have had for waiting until 1895 to publish his criticisms? How might Murphy's role as a missionary have shaped his testimony?

When I left [Equatorville in May] the people were in a very unsettled condition and most unfriendly to the State. The revolt which had broken out throughout the Aruwhimi [Aruwimi] district in consequence of the tyranny of the State officers in regard to the rubber traffic had been quelled, but not until the State troops, which had been forced to retire upon Basoko and to withstand a siege there, had been reinforced. Scarcely, however, had the steamers which had been sent to the relief of the station returned to Stanley Pool before two were again despatched—during the months of June and July—to quell another disturbance which had broken out at Luluaburg [Luluabourg] on the Kasai. This time it was a revolt of the State troops against their own officers. The soldiers killed one and wounded another, leaving him for dead upon the field. They then looted the station and escaped into the interior. Although the authorities sent up a strong detachment of forces from Stanley Pool and commenced hostilities on a large scale, most of the fugitives are still at large. . . .

The attitude of the natives of the Congo Free State is everywhere unfriendly, and if the people do not universally rebel against authority it is because they are reduced to a state of despair. If possible they leave the territory. Two of the most flourishing towns in Mr. H. M. Stanley's time, situated at Stanley Pool, viz,—Kintamo and Kinchassa [Kinshasa]—are now no more, and the people have gone over to the French Congo. Besides the natives of towns I have named many people have left the main river and gone into the interior in order to escape the arbitrary demands of the State. Difficulties have arisen, too, between the State and the porters, and if the requisite number of carriers were not forthcoming detachments of soldiers were sent with orders to capture all the women they could find. Several Christians were arrested in this manner. The natives and missionaries remonstrated, and presented a letter to the Governor without getting any redress. The people were so enraged at these outrages that they took matters into their own hands. They killed three white men and met and defeated the State forces in more than one pitched engagement. On the Lower Congo the natives have good Snider rifles, and their many conflicts with the State have taught them the arts of war. In some of the fights the State soldiers could not see their foes as the latter were in ambush. The result was that they were just mowed down by their opponents' guns.

Mr. Murphy next proceeded to give incidents of the barbarities alleged to have been perpetrated by the State for the purpose of obtaining rubber. He said:

I have seen these things done, and have remonstrated with the State in the years 1888, 1889, and 1894, but never got satisfaction. I have been in the interior and have seen the ravages made by the State in pursuit of this iniquitous trade. In one place I stood by the side of the river, and heard a little boy describe how he had seen the Belgians shoot people for not fetching rubber, and at the same time he pointed to the flagstaff to which the poor victims had been tied, and which still bore the bullet and blood marks. Let me give an incident to show how this unrighteous trade affects the people. One day a State corporal, who was in charge of the post of Lolifa, was going round the town collecting rubber. Meeting a poor woman whose husband was away fishing, he said, "Where is your husband?" She answered by pointing to the river. He then said, "Where is his rubber?" She answered, "It is ready for you," whereupon he said, "You lie," and, lifting his gun, shot her dead. Shortly afterwards the husband returned, and was told of the murder of his wife. He went straight to the corporal, taking with him his rubber, and asked why he had shot his wife. The wretched man then raised his gun and killed the corporal. The soldiers ran away to the headquarters of the State, made misrepresentations of the case, with the result that the commissaire sent a large force to support the authority of the soldiers; the town was looted, burned, and many people killed and wounded. In November last there was heavy fighting upon the Bosira, because the people refused to give rubber, and I was told upon the authority of a State officer that no fewer than 1,890 people were killed. Upon another occasion, in the month of November, 1894, some soldiers ran away from a State steamer and, it was said, went to the town of Bompanga. The State sent a message telling the chief of the town to give them up. He answered that he could not, as the fugitives had not been in his town. The State sent the messenger a second time with the order—"Come to me at once, or war in the morning." The next morning the old chief went to meet the Belgians and was attacked without provocation. He himself was wounded, his wife killed before his eyes, and her head cut off that they might possess the brass necklet that she wore. Twenty-four of the chief's people were also killed, and all for the paltry reason given above. Again, the people of Lake Mantumba [Lake Tumba] ran away on account of the cruelty of the State, and the latter sent some soldiers in charge of a coloured corporal to treat with them and induce them to return. On the way the troops met a canoe containing seven of the fugitives. Under some paltry pretext they made the people land, shot them, cut off their hands, and took them to the commissaire. The Mantumba people complained to the missionary at Irebu, and he went down to see if the story was true. He ascertained the case to be just as they had narrated, and found that one of the seven was a little girl who was not quite dead. The child recovered and she lives to-day, the stump of the handless arm witnessing against this horrible practice. These are only a few things of many that have taken place in one district. . . .

. . . The State is strong enough to-day to do these things because the people lack unity. They have no leaders, no common cause, and no weapons to fight. Their condition is indeed deplorable, and needs our sympathy, as well as all that European public opinion can do to secure for them the blessings of a righteous government under which they can live in peace.

Regarding the State officers and their manner of administration, Mr. Murphy said:—

. . . It is impossible for the Governor at Boma—four weeks' journey from Stanley Pool, which ought to be the real seat of Government—to manage his vast and unwieldy territory, so that the commissaires and petty governors of the interior districts have almost unlimited power. The officers of the State are young and inexperienced; they do not come out as colonists to develop the country, but in order that they may receive quick promotion, the Congo decoration, and, above all, to get money. Of course there are some noble exceptions, but it is only the few who have an interest in the country and in the well-being of the people. I have been told by naval and other officers of the State that a certain sum per head is paid by the Government to the commissaires of districts from which slaves are received, and to the naval officers who bring them into camp. These wretched slaves soon find they have only changed masters. About 50 per cent are in starving condition.

Let me . . . again just revert to the rubber question, which is by far the most pressing, being accountable for most of the horrors perpetrated on the Congo. It has reduced the people to a state of utter despair. Each town in the district is forced to bring a certain quantity to the head-quarters of the commissaire every Sunday. It is collected by force. The soldiers drive the people into the bush. If they will not go they are shot down, and their left hands cut off and taken as trophies to the commissaire. The soldiers do not care who they shoot down, and they more often shoot poor helpless women and harmless children. These hands, the hands of men, women, and children, are placed in rows before the commissaire, who counts them to see that the soldiers have not wasted the cartridges. The commissaire is paid a commission of about 1d. [1 penny] a pound upon all the rubber he gets. It is therefore to his interest to get as much as he can.

16

THE REVEREND E. V. SJÖBLOM

Testimony

May 14, 1897

The Reverend E. V. Sjöblom was a Swedish member of the American Baptist Missionary Union who had already worked for five years in Congo when he gave this testimony. He was one of the first missionaries to speak publicly in Great Britain against the Congo Free State, in a speech to the Aborigines' Protection Society in London in 1897. He gave the interview excerpted here during the same visit to England. His account of the cutting off of hands by sentries and soldiers as a means of accounting for spent cartridges and people killed was subsequently challenged in a letter to the editor of The Times *of London by the governor-general of the Congo Free State, Baron Théophile Wahis (Document 17). Sjöblom refers to a massacre and a subsequent inquiry by Wahis that are recounted in the oral history by Antoine Boongo (Document 11). What questions or issues should a historian consider in cross-referencing or combining the information of a contemporary source such as Sjöblom's interview with that of an oral history such as Boongo's, recorded sixty years later?*

At the end of last year a force of State soldiers at the order of the commissaire of the [Equateur] district entered the village of Mandaka Vajigo [Vagigo], near my station, and, seeing the natives run away as usual at their approach, held out a quantity of brass rods with which they trade, indicating that they were not there to fight, but to buy food. Seeing their pacific

"Affairs on the Upper Congo," *The Times* (London), May 14, 1897.

intentions the natives returned and commenced to prepare the food. Meanwhile a portion of the troops were sent down to the other end of the village, the natives were surrounded, the State soldiers opened fire upon them, and about 50 were killed. This being reported to us by the soldiers and the natives, Mr. Banks rode out to inquire into it. He himself counted 20 or 30 dead bodies, and the natives wanted him to go into the bush, where they said many more were lying. Mr. Banks, having seen the bodies in the village and a heap of hands that had been cut off, concluded he had ample proof without going into the bush. He seemed surprised that the hands had not been sent to the State station to be counted, but was told that it was not necessary to show them to the State officer; they were counted by the native sergeant. A few days later Governor Wahis on his return down river called in at our station and asked Mr. Banks if any further atrocities had taken place since his last visit. Mr. Banks detailed what he had heard, and M. Wahis answered that it was impossible. He told the Governor that he had seen it himself, whereupon M. Wahis summoned the commandant in charge—the officer who had ordered the raid had already gone elsewhere—and asked him in French if the story was true. The Belgian officer assured M. Wahis that it was, but the latter, thinking Mr. Banks did not understand French, said, "After all you may have seen this, but you have no witnesses." "Oh," said Mr. Banks, "I can call the commandant, who has just told you it is true." M. Wahis then tried to minimize the matter, when to his great surprise Mr. Banks added, "In any case I have at his own request furnished to the British Consul who passed through here lately a signed statement concerning it."

M. Wahis rose from his chair, saying, "Oh, then it is all over Europe." Then for the first time he said that the responsible commissaire must be punished. Some time after the Governor's departure we were surprised to hear that the guilty officer had been sentenced to five years' imprisonment. As the officer was all this time waging warfare in the interior we failed to understand what it meant. We afterwards learnt that he had been sentenced to remain for five years on the Congo, without furlough.

Mr. Sjöblom went on to show that "the curse of the Congo is its forced labour," especially in connexion with the collection of rubber. "Native armed sentinels chosen from the wildest tribes are placed in the towns to force the people to bring in rubber." In illustration of the horrors of this system. Mr. Sjöblom related the following incidents, of which he had been an eyewitness:—

In February, 1895, while I was preaching to a number of natives at a place called Ebira, where a white man had never been seen before, some of these sentinels rushed forward and seized an old man because he had been away fishing instead of collecting rubber. The old man was thrown to the ground and dragged a few yards aside. The sentinel then pointed the gun at his head and shot him there before my eyes. Then, putting another cartridge into his gun, he pointed it at the crowd and they immediately fled. Next he told a little boy, eight or nine years old, to cut off the old man's right hand, which he did. The dying man, not yet quite insensible, attempted to withdraw his hand when he felt the knife, but in vain. The hand was then placed on a fallen tree, where already four others were displayed, so that all might see them and take warning. The others had previously been smoked, and shortly this, too, was laid on the fire and smoked, in order to preserve them for the commissaire—trophies of civilization. Besides what I have seen on my journeys, sentinels have often passed the mission station carrying smoked hands, which were being taken to the commissaire with the rubber. The latest date on which this occurred in my sight was December 14, 1895, when I, together with two other missionaries, saw a sentinel pass carrying a basket containing 18 right hands. From the size of them we could tell that they had belonged to men, women, and children. The hands were placed on the ground and counted.

"There were 19 hands," exclaimed the sentinel, turning in anger to the woman who carried the basket, "how is it you have lost one?" The woman had been captured for the purpose of carrying the basket, which very likely contained the hands of her own relatives. We could not understand how it was that these murders were still going on when we had heard that the commissaire had given orders to the sentinels that no more people were to be killed on account of the rubber business. But on my last journey, December, 1895, I discovered the secret. One Monday night a sentinel, having just delivered his amount of rubber to the commissaire, came to me asking my advice. "What are we to do?" he said. "When all the people are gathered together the commissaire openly tells us sentinels not to kill any more people for the rubber. 'If you do I will kill you, or send you to Boma,' but afterwards he calls us aside and privately tells us 'If the people do not bring plenty of rubber kill some, but do not bring any more hands to me; never mind my command.'"

Other sentinels came to me in the same perplexity. They were simply the commissaire's tools, and liable to be put to death for killing others, as a means of justifying himself; and in equal danger of losing their lives for not bringing in the full amount of rubber at the cost of bloodshed.

17

GOVERNOR-GENERAL THÉOPHILE WAHIS

Letter to the Editor

May 31, 1897

Théophile Wahis (1844–1921) began his career as an army officer. He was the governor-general of the Congo Free State between 1892 and 1908, then of the Belgian Congo between 1908 and 1912. For his service to the state, Leopold II elevated him to the noble rank of baron in 1901. In this selection, he refutes the charges by the Reverends John Murphy (Document 15) and E. V. Sjöblom (Document 16) on the basis of his tour of Congo in 1896–1897. This tour and its consequences are recalled in the oral histories by Antoine Boongo (Document 11) and Balofo Is'a Mboyo and Ekombe Is'ek'Ombola (Document 12). Wahis mentions his recent creation of the "Commission for the protection of aborigines," which was intended to assist the state in ensuring the well-being of the Congolese. This commission included prominent Catholic missionaries, and its secretary was the Reverend George Grenfell of the Baptist Missionary Society, who was then the most famous Protestant missionary in Congo. The commission was designed to pit Protestant and Catholic missionaries against each other in their criticism or defense of the state, a tactic seen elsewhere in Wahis's letter to the editor. He was generally suspicious of Protestants as agents of the British government, and he regularly invoked the testimony of Catholic missionaries, who did not participate in the public criticism of the state, perhaps because the state gave them preferential treatment. Do the oral histories by Boongo and Is'a Mboyo and Is'ek'Ombola support or contradict Wahis's claims?

Sir,—On my return to Europe several articles on Congolese affairs recently published in the English Press were placed before my eyes, and particularly an interview of a missionary, Mr. Sjöblom, who attacked me personally.

I will not leave the accusations drawn up against the agents of the State without an answer.

Théophile Wahis, "The Congo State," letter to the editor, *The Times* (London), May 31, 1897.

During the inspection tour which I have just taken in the districts of the interior I had the occasion to examine their administration, to see how the natives were treated, to meet with most of the missionaries; and I declare formally that it is downright dishonesty to represent the agents of the State as inhuman and cruel to the native populations.

If there have been individual abuses, like everywhere, I have ascertained that the instructions given by the Government to its agents as to their relations with the natives, have, on the whole, been executed.

I will examine Mr. Sjöblom's accusations successively.

To begin with, he takes up ancient facts pointed to by the Rev. Mr. Murphy in *The Times* of November 18, 1895. As soon as these facts came to my knowledge by that number of the paper — for the missionaries on the spot never gave any notice of them to either the judicial authorities or myself — I ordered the matter to be investigated and an inquiry was made in February, 1896, by Judge De Lancker.

This inquiry reduced Mr. Murphy's allegations to little more than nothing. Thus, not one witness was found to confirm the supposed murder of a native woman by a soldier at the post of Lolifa; thus, again, it was proved that the mutilation of which a little girl had been the victim had been perpetrated by a native, who was condemned to five years' penal servitude for that crime. As to the alleged attack in November, 1894, on the village of Bompanga "without any kind of provocation," I have ascertained that the operation against that village had been brought about by acts of insubordination.

When in Coquilhatville in November, 1896, I took the initiative of an interview with Messrs. Banks and Sjöblom about the facts to which the Rev. Mr. Murphy had drawn the attention of the public, and I informed them of the result of the inquiries. I must oppose a formal denial to the fanciful account Mr. Sjöblom gives of our interview. Mr. Sjöblom says that I refused to hear evidence from natives whom he had brought to his house in order to bear witness to the truth of a fact of which he accused some soldiers.

The point in question was precisely to ascertain whether in the Bompanga affair the five soldiers sent to arrest a chief who refused to present himself before the District Commissioner had attacked the natives or if the latter had tried to prevent the arrestation and thus brought about an aggression.

I told Mr. Sjöblom that a minute inquiry had already been made into the subject, that from the whole of the depositions and the examination of the circumstances a conclusion had been arrived at that the five soldiers who had found themselves before great numbers of natives had done nothing but return an attack.

I added that the natives collected by Mr. Sjöblom were evidently those who had declared the soldiers to have been aggressors in the first instance, that I knew, therefore, what they were going to tell me, and that [based on] the facts, dating from more than 18 months ago and having been investigated in the presence of Europeans and natives whose responsibility was engaged, there was evidently no cause for another inquest.

With a curious obstinacy Mr. Sjöblom constantly came back to accusations which had already been examined at different times. He did not furnish me with any particulars useful to the investigation I wished to make, but evidently showed the unkind feelings he entertained towards our agents. It was then I told him that he was himself accused by numerous natives of exciting the populations to resist the orders of the authorities, that the accusations seemed founded, and made him thus liable to be prosecuted.

I may here add that, if Mr. Sjöblom was not actually prosecuted, it was precisely because under the circumstances proceedings against him might have appeared like retaliation, and it seemed desirable to avoid this.

In his recent interview Mr. Sjöblom denounces new facts; 45 villages have been set on fire. Where? When? By whom?

A native was killed by a soldier at Ebira in February, 1895; and the Rev. Mr. Banks, Mr. Sjöblom's superior, who has lived at Bolengi [Bolenge] since 1887, and whose testimony will certainly not be suspected, has declared on oath that until March, 1895, he never had one complaint to make.

Mr. Sjöblom has seen natives' hands cut off. It has undoubtedly happened that soldiers have cut off the hands of killed enemies after a fight. The mutilation of corpses is a custom that exists or has existed in almost every part of Africa. A warrior brings in hands or heads which he has cut off as a proof of his valour. In the Congo State more than in many other countries efforts are being made to bring about the disappearance of these abominable practices. Penal law declares them a crime, and punishes any mutilation of corpses with penal servitude for terms varying from two months to two years. Here is a recent instruction given on the matter:—

> Many of our soldiers do not know that they commit an offence when they cut off a limb from a dead enemy; officers must, in consequence,

often impress them with their horror of such practices. Each time a soldier arrives at a post new representations must be made to him. Constantly repeated warnings alone can bring about the disappearance of a barbarous custom which provokes our indignation.

If it was noticed that commanders of troops did not fulfill the duties imposed upon them by the present instruction, they would make themselves liable to disciplinary penalties for the offences committed by their soldiers.

Of all the facts cited by Mr. Sjöblom, only one had been proved true, and yet it was surrounded by this missionary with false circumstances. I am speaking of the Mandaka Vagigo affair. It is true that this village, having refused to pay the tax, had to be repressed in October, 1896. The inhabitants resisted and lost a certain number of men. The repression was legitimate in itself; but, contrary to the instructions, a mistake was made in giving the command of the troop to a black sergeant. Mr. Sjöblom gives to understand that the guilty officer was not punished; he was revoked.

It is absolutely false that I made up my mind to take steps against him only after I heard the facts were known to the English Consul, who had just passed through Coquilhatville. Mr. Sjöblom knows very well that I became aware of this on my return to this locality only. I reproached Mr. Banks with not having informed me of the facts sooner, thus forgetting his promise to let me hear at once any complaint he might have to make against any of our agents.

. . . It was only after begging Mr. Banks to come and see me, and questioning him, that I learned what had happened. On the very same day I took a disciplinary measure against the accused officer, and the latter was revoked as soon as the necessary formalities had been gone through.

I often was sorry to notice that the authority did not find in some of the missionaries the help upon which it is justified in counting. In every conversation I had with them during my last journey up the river, I had to insist on their duty of acquainting us with any illegal facts that might come to their knowledge.

On August 7 last I wrote to one of them:—

If you noticed that natives were the victims to violence of any kind, you would render the District Commissioner a service by exposing the facts to him, but it is of importance that you should investigate the matter yourself first, and avoid simply repeating vague allegations made by natives who often have not even witnessed the facts of which they talk.

When Europeans, either private individuals or agents of the State, are the authors of violence against natives, an inquiry always takes place and they are prosecuted. I do not wish to conceal the fact that I have had to fulfil this painful duty now and then, for I do not pretend that no abuse of power has ever taken place; but punishment has always followed.

I accuse Mr. Sjöblom of giving credit to the opinion that the authorities shut their eyes on offences perpetrated by their agents.

The Congo Administration only wishes to throw a light upon these offences, and, in this respect, I consider the institution of the Commission for the protection of aborigines, which I had to organize lately, as a beneficent measure.

I am convinced that the Government has not appealed in vain to such men as Monseigneur van Ronalé, [Misters] Grenfell and Sims, and the [Reverend Fathers] Van Henexthoven and De Cleene; every one of them has accepted the humanitarian mission which was intrusted to them. The secretary of the Commission, the Rev. Mr. Grenfell, expected them to meet at Leopoldville in May, and on his suggestion some members will be added to the Commission. I have noticed by the letters which some of these gentlemen have addressed to me that they are among those who render justice to the efforts of the State. Father Van Honexthoven, of the Jesuits, wrote:—

> I must in truth declare that during the four years I have spent in the Stanley Pool's district I have never noticed an act of violence worth being reported to the authorities. I have always found in the district commissioners a spirit of justice and equity in keeping with the important functions they fulfilled.

And Mr. Grenfell says:—

> I am happy to believe that some of the reports are quite untrue. Certainly some of the last published revelations reach me for the first time through the newspapers. I am convinced that in each of the districts where our society (B.M.S.) is represented by a station the rule of the State is infinitely more beneficent than any native regime I have known, and that life and property are more and increasingly secure.

During my last voyage I confirmed to our agents the Government's instructions as to the manner in which natives should be treated. For instance, I wrote to the Commissioner of the Lake Leopold district on January 9 last:—

> The Government has given orders that natives should be always and everywhere treated with the utmost humanity. These orders do not

imply that you should abstain from taking measures in order to force the populations to pay the taxes, light enough, to which they are submitted. Where the natives obstinately refuse to work, you will force them to do so by taking hostages. Arms must be resorted to only in case of resistance and when the safety of the troop is compromised. You will take care that all your agents shall know their duties in this respect. The little posts commanded by black sergeants shall be under the strictest supervision. Their doings must be constantly controlled.

In every district I have ordered those in command of posts to listen carefully to complaints from the natives and to pay the latter regularly and directly for their produce. On April 1 last I wrote to the Commissioner of the Equator:—

It is impossible to suppress every little soldiers' post, but your constant effort must tend to narrowly watch them, and each time you will notice that soldiers have committed exactions among the populations where they are placed you must take repressive measures with the greatest severity.

It is not for me to state the progress made by the Congo State since its origin, or the remarkable results obtained as much from the point of view of material progress as from that of the amelioration of the social and moral condition of the native population. But as the chief of the local Government it is my duty to protest aloud against the insults of which Belgian officers have been the object. I have seen them at work, I have known the hardships of their task, I have appreciated the high sense they have of their duties, and I am proud to say that the officers in the Congo service have maintained their claims to esteem and respect.

I am, Sir, your obedient servant,
WAHIS

Bruxelles May 29.

18

Circular to All District Commissioners, Heads of Zones and of Posts [of the Congo Free State], with Regard to Barbarous Customs Prevailing among the Native Tribes

February 27, 1897

This official circular, dispatched from Brussels, exemplifies the Congo Free State's condemnation of "barbarous customs" such as cannibalism and the use of ordeal by poison in witch hunts. The state publicized its prosecution of cannibals in courts run by the Department of Criminal Justice to demonstrate its commitment to the civilizing mission. This circular, issued in 1897, declares that the state has become sufficiently strong to act decisively to end such customs and "enforce absolute respect for the Penal Law." Although there is no reference to this cultural reform campaign in any of the Congolese accounts of this period in the eastern Congo and Equateur District, one might speculate that perhaps the circular had greater effect between the coast and Stanley Pool, where state officials and troops were concentrated. Given that most state officials in the upper Congo surely ignored this circular, why did officials in Brussels write and send it?

GENTLEMEN,

As you are aware, the Government have had constantly under their consideration the barbarous practices, such as cannibalism, ordeal by poison, and human sacrifices, which prevail among the native tribes, and the best means of bringing about their disappearance.

In this matter, as in all questions in which allowance must to some extent be made for long-established custom and social conditions which it would be impolitic to attack too directly, the Government have thought it advisable to act at first with prudence and circumspection, without, however, remaining inactive.

Henry Wellington Wack, *The Story of the Congo Free State* (New York: G. P. Putnam's Sons, 1905), 566–68.

For this reason the first instruction[s] issued to officers did not, in all cases, prescribe repression by force; they enjoined the exercise of their influence and authority with a view to deterring the natives by persuasion from indulging in these inhuman practices. A further advance has been made: the moment the authority of the State was sufficiently established in the neighbourhood of its posts and stations, the toleration of such customs was formally prohibited within a certain distance round the State stations or European establishments, and the Penal Law made their repression in these places possible by its provisions respecting acts of violence against the person. Outside this limit it lay with the officers of the Department of Criminal Justice (*Ministère Public*) to prosecute or not, according as the situation of the district and the forces at the disposal of the authorities permitted.

These measures have not been without result. Not only have cases of cannibalism become less frequent in the centres occupied by the officers of the State, but the native himself has learnt, and now knows, the horror felt by Europeans for cannibalism, and is no longer ignorant of the fact that by giving way to it he renders himself liable to punishment. As a general rule, indeed, it is only in secret, and out of sight of Europeans, that he still indulges in the odious custom, for he has become convinced that, save in exceptional cases in which the white man is powerless to do otherwise, he will not let him go unpunished.

The Government considers that an even more decisive step should be taken in the direction of repression. As the State's occupation of these districts becomes more and more complete, as its posts are multiplied all along the Upper Congo, and as regular Courts are gaining a footing in the interior, the moment seems to have come to endeavour to reach the evil once for all, and to seek to extirpate it everywhere where our authority is sufficiently established to enable us to enforce absolute respect for the Penal Law.

It was with this view that the Decree of the 18th December, 1896, was drawn up, by which more particularly cases of cannibalism and ordeal by poison were made special offences. It is the Government's intention that these provisions shall be strictly enforced, and it is the aim of the present Circular to direct all our officers to bring to justice any offences of this kind which may come to their knowledge. It will be the duty of the officers of the Department of Criminal Justice (*Ministère Public*) to institute proceedings against the delinquents, and in these special cases they will not be at liberty to apply Article 84 of the Decree of the 27th April, 1889, and to hand them over to the jurisdiction of the local Chief to be dealt with by native custom. It is, indeed, evident that such a course is out of the question in dealing with a class of offences which are contrary to the principles of our civilisation, and which are the outcome of customs which we are seeking to abolish.

The Government count on general assistance, with a view to insuring the prompt and certain repression of these offences, and they believe that a few severe examples will have a powerful effect in inducing the native to put an end to these reprehensible practices. The District Commissioners and Heads of Stations are in this connection expected to police the territories under their administration, and to take the necessary measures to obtain exact information.

The Director of Justice will forward to the Government every quarter a Report on the practice of cannibalism, on the cases prosecuted, and, if necessary, on the new measures which should be taken in order to check and extirpate this custom.

19

FEDERATION FOR THE DEFENSE OF BELGIAN INTERESTS ABROAD

Taxation of the Natives
February 15, 1905

This article appeared in the periodical The Truth about the Congo (La Vérité sur le Congo), *the primary organ of Congo Free State propaganda in Europe. This periodical was published by the Federation for the Defense of Belgian Interests Abroad, a nominal organization created at Leopold II's command in 1903 to distribute ostensibly impartial information about Congo. Significantly, Governor-General Théophile Wahis was a vice president of the federation and an editor of this periodical. The contents were printed in parallel columns in English, French, and German, and the issues were distributed throughout Europe, commonly on the seats of trains. This article demonstrates one of the Congo Free State's common propaganda tactics: It asserts that the state's administrative policies were identical to those of other imperial powers in Africa. Specifically, the article*

Federation for the Defense of Belgian Interests Abroad, "Taxation of the Natives," *The Truth about the Congo*, February 15, 1905, 58–61.

equates Congo Free State policies with those of Britain's Uganda Protec-
torate, among other British territories. Harry Johnston (Document 4)
instituted those policies in Uganda as a British imperial official. The
article refutes criticisms made by the secretary of the Congo Reform Asso-
ciation in Britain, Edmund Morel (Document 21), who charged that
the state's taxation, enforced by punitive expeditions, constituted a new
system of slavery. Does this article define limits of the state's authority to
tax Congolese peoples? Can you reconcile this argument on behalf of the
Congo Free State's system of taxation with the principles of the civilizing
mission?

If the abominable criticisms raised against our colonial undertaking lead
to some good, it is in the way of drawing attention to often disregarded
questions and of indirectly contributing to throw a little light upon them.
Such is the case with the problem of the taxation of the natives. People
who are content to read newspapers have no idea of the considerable
difficulty which the collection of taxes involves and do not, therefore,
show the slightest indulgence for the errors or abuses that are liable to
take place in spite of the best intentions of the Governments and their
agents. The Secretary of the Congo Reform Association can be said to
have cleverly imposed upon that ignorance which is quite natural in the
case of the persons unacquainted with the details of administration of an
African colony.

Are the Natives to Be Taxed?

The reply is, generally speaking, affirmative and we do not think that
even the Secretary of the Congo Reform Association would reply otherwise. In any case the tax-payers in Europe, be they French, German or
English, would answer yes and they would in this respect agree with the
cleverest administrators of colonies and theorists of colonisation.

In his book on the Uganda Protectorate, Sir Harry Johnston
writes: — "The general theory being that the native pays for the protection which he receives, if native chiefs are unable to so govern their
people as to ensure peace and quiet in their countries and protection
to foreigners, thereby obliging the Administration of the Protectorate
to intervene, they must pay hut and gun taxes as the result of not being
able to manage their own affairs."

Nor does the difficulty lie there. For some years past, the various
colonial Governments in Africa have instituted more or less complete

systems of taxation. And it will be a matter of interest to know the nature of the taxes and the way of levying them.

What Are the Proper Taxes to Levy?

The tax is collected either in cash, kind or labour.

Of the above three methods, the first is, in our opinion, the worst because the native has generally no money and must accordingly not be asked for any. Sir Harry Johnston, whom we like to quote on account of his great competency, wrote in his book on the Uganda Protectorate that "even supposing the entire male population of the Protectorate was ready to pay taxes, they have not at present the money with which to pay them."

This very obvious reason does not prevent the English from exacting money from the natives in several of their colonies, as for instance in Nyassaland [Nyasaland]. The consequence of such a system is to compel the native to take service with a European planter in order to earn the tax he has to pay over to the Treasury.

Taxation in this colony, moreover, amounts to nothing more than a scarcely disguised proceeding employed with the view of providing British contractors with labour. So true is this that the natives having after a while succeeded in selling their own produce, this trade was there and then nipped in the bud: the amount of the tax was doubled so as to compel the natives to return to the plantations of the colonists.

Taxation in kind and taxation in labour are practically two variations of one and the same system. In both cases, it is in reality taxing the physical strength of the natives. The better plan is to make the law agree with economic reality and to decide that the tax shall in principle be reckoned and paid in labour. The Congo State has not lost sight of this clear rule of sound colonial Administration.

What Is the Best Way of Levying the Tax?

This is a matter which gives rise to the greatest difficulties.

Prior to levying the tax it is necessary to assess it and at the present time such an assessment cannot, in any colony of tropical Africa, be based on a complete census of the population. Nowhere in this region does a census exist and nowhere has it been possible, so far, to make one. It is necessary that the heads of districts and other agents charged with the collection of taxes should perform their duty in an exceptionally cautious manner so that in spite of their best endeavours, certain villages be not over-taxed whilst others are comparatively under-rated.

If an agent who was expected to render good service, degenerates in the midst of isolation and under the African climate; if, out of sheer laziness, he prefers to avoid travelling about and to exact the whole tax from the villages in close proximity to his post; if, finally, such abuse takes place unbeknown to the authorities and notwithstanding all their efforts to prevent it, the Government cannot, in fairness, be held responsible.

What means of compulsion are to be resorted to if the natives refuse to pay the taxes?

The famous Ordinance of 1897, levying a Hut Tax in Sierra Leone points out, as means of compulsion, the seizure of the tax payers, real estates and movables, and the sale of the latter by auction.

Such a proceedure is the most delusive one that could possibly be imagined, inasmuch as in Africa there generally exists no market or outlet for the sale of forfeited property. Then again, such property is frequently the joint property of the natives. Under those circumstances, how can it be seized and sold?

That is why the above system, which as a matter of fact is inapplicable, has not in reality been applied. The sanguinary incidents which were the outcome of the levy of the tax in Sierra-Leone are within recollection.

In practice, it seems that in the British Colonies, the ordinary means of compulsion resorted to against uncomplying subjects is that of *punitive expeditions*, an echo of which reaches us from the *West Coast* by almost every mail. A practically continuous rumour of war comes from that part; the newspapers publish notes running for instance thus: "The promptness with which the expedition set out caused a panic among the natives, who took to flight. *Five stockades were burnt.*" (*Times*, November 22nd 1904, wired from Bathurst, Gambia.) In this case, it was a question of compelling a chief to surrender an offender. But, whatever may have been the particular cause of the "punitive expedition" referred to, this brief information says a good deal as to the treatment of the natives.

In some colonies, considerable premiums (10 and even 20%) on the taxes received are allotted to the native Chiefs having the collection under their control. What methods do the Chiefs resort to in compelling their subjects? This is not stated, but it stands to reason that such a "system" is likely to lead to serious misuse, if a close watch is not kept upon its application.

The petty native princes have an evident and direct interest in exhausting their subjects. They are unavoidably supported by the authorities. And experience proves that the native chiefs charged with levying the tax are "general farmers" as a rule less deserving of confidence than white agents.

The system usually resorted to by the colonial Governments is compulsion, also called forced labour. By a perhaps unintentional misuse of the terms, certain opponents of ours call it "system of hostages." Like all systems, it is liable to give rise to abuses. Still they are in our opinion less serious than those resulting from the system of *punitive expeditions*, which are in reality *war* turned into a way of governing.

Those who so passionately denounce the "Congolese system" pass a wholesale and indiscriminate criticism upon a most intricate legal and economical structure. This "system" consists of a great many parts. As a proof that it works well, taken altogether, we have the marvellous development of the Congo State, which the natives are the first to derive advantage from. That partial improvements can be made there is possible, because such is usually the case with human undertakings. Even British colonial policy does not escape and it is most unfair to pass nothing but condemning judgments when the Belgian Congo is involved whilst, on the other hand, so many things are overlooked when the matter concerns Sierra Leone, Nigeria, South Africa . . . or Western Australia!

20

JOHN HOBSON

From Imperialism: A Study

1902

John A. Hobson (1858–1940) was a leading British liberal social theorist and advocate of internationalist cooperation and governance. In Imperialism: A Study*, his wide-ranging critique of the new imperialism in Africa and Asia, he asserts that financiers and industrialists are exerting undue influence on governments' foreign policies in order to secure new overseas markets and opportunities for investment at the expense of poorly paid workers and democracy at home. Moreover, Hobson was critical of imperialism for subjugating and exploiting the "lower races" instead of improving them. He compared the Congo Free State with imperialist regimes elsewhere, as can be seen in his critical references to British*

J. A. Hobson, *Imperialism: A Study* (1902; repr., London: George Allen & Unwin, 1948), 12–13, 48–49, 59–61, 253–54, 256–57, 279–80.

territories. In this excerpt, he refers to the "trust" that the "superior races"
(whites) hold over their imperial subjects. At that time, the principle of
"trusteeship" was understood as a proper paternalistic relationship in
which the superior races looked after the property and welfare of the lower
races in the latter's presumed best interest. Hobson's arguments represent
some of the most influential criticisms of the new imperialism and echo
the views of Edmund Morel, secretary of the Congo Reform Association
(see Document 21). What are Hobson's views on the civilizing mission?
Do you see his economic critique of imperialism reflected in recent or cur-
rent debates over international foreign policy and military intervention?

The scramble for Africa and Asia virtually recast the policy of all European nations, evoked alliances which cross all natural lines of sympathy
and historical association, drove every continental nation to consume an
ever-growing share of its material and human resources upon military
and naval equipment, drew the great new power of the United States
from its isolation into the full tide of competition; and, by the multitude,
the magnitude, and the suddenness of the issues it had thrown on to the
stage of politics, became a constant agent of menace and of perturba-
tion to the peace and progress of mankind. The new policy exercised the
most notable and formidable influence upon the conscious statecraft of
the nations which indulge in it. While producing for popular consumption
doctrines of national destiny and imperial missions of civilization, contra-
dictory in their true import, but subsidiary to one another as supports
of popular Imperialism, it evoked a calculating, greedy type of Machia-
vellianism, entitled "real-politik" in Germany, where it was made, which
remodelled the whole art of diplomacy and erected national aggrandise-
ment without pity or scruple as the conscious motive force of foreign
policy. Earth hunger and the scramble for markets were responsible
for the openly avowed repudiation of treaty obligations which Germany,
Russia, and England had not scrupled to defend. The sliding scale of
diplomatic language, hinterland, sphere of interest, sphere of influence,
paramountcy, suzerainty, protectorate, veiled or open, leading up to acts
of forcible seizure or annexation which sometimes continue to be hidden
under "lease," "rectification of frontier," "concession," and the like, was
the invention and expression of this cynical spirit of Imperialism. . . .

What is the direct economic outcome of Imperialism? A great expenditure of public money upon ships, guns, military and naval equipment
and stores, growing and productive of enormous profits when a war, or an
alarm of war, occurs; new public loans and important fluctuations in the

home and foreign Bourses [stock exchanges]; more posts for soldiers and sailors and in the diplomatic and consular services; improvement of foreign investments by the substitution of the British flag for a foreign flag; acquisition of markets for certain classes of exports, and some protection and assistance for British trades in these manufactures; employment for engineers, missionaries, speculative miners, ranchers and other emigrants.

Certain definite business and professional interests feeding upon imperialistic expenditure, or upon the results of that expenditure, are thus set up in opposition to the common good, and, instinctively feeling their way to one another, are found united in strong sympathy to support every new imperialist exploit.

If the £60,000,000 which may now be taken as a minimum expenditure on armaments in time of peace were subjected to a close analysis, most of it would be traced directly to the tills of certain big firms engaged in building warships and transports, equipping and coaling them, manufacturing guns, rifles, ammunition, 'planes and motor vehicles of every kind, supplying horses, waggons, saddlery, food, clothing for the services, contracting for barracks, and for other large irregular needs. Through these main channels the millions flow to feed many subsidiary trades, most of which are quite aware that they are engaged in executing contracts for the services. Here we have an important nucleus of commercial Imperialism. Some of these trades, especially the shipbuilding, boilermaking, and gun and ammunition making trades, are conducted by large firms with immense capital, whose heads are well aware of the uses of political influence for trade purposes.

These men are Imperialists by conviction; a pushful policy is good for them. . . .

. . . Finance is the governor of the imperial engine, directing the energy and determining its work: it does not constitute the fuel of the engine, nor does it directly generate the power. Finance manipulates the patriotic forces which politicians, soldiers, philanthropists, and traders generate; the enthusiasm for expansion which issues from these sources, though strong and genuine, is irregular and blind; the financial interest has those qualities of concentration and clear-sighted calculation which are needed to set Imperialism to work. An ambitious statesman, a frontier soldier, an overzealous missionary, a pushing trader, may suggest or even initiate a step of imperial expansion, may assist in educating patriotic public opinion to the urgent need of some fresh advance, but the final determination rests with the financial power. The direct influence exercised by great financial houses in "high politics" is supported by the control which they exercise over the body of public opinion through the Press, which, in every "civilised" country, is becoming more and more their obedient instrument. While the specifically financial newspaper imposes "facts" and "opinions" on the business classes, the general body of the Press comes more and more under the conscious or unconscious domination of financiers. . . .

Such is the array of distinctively economic forces making for Imperialism. . . .

The play of these forces does not openly appear. They are essentially parasites upon patriotism, and they adapt themselves to its protecting colours. In the mouth of their representatives are noble phrases, expressive of their desire to extend the area of civilisation, to establish good government, promote Christianity, extirpate slavery, and elevate the lower races. . . .

Whenever superior races settle on lands where lower races can be profitably used for manual labour in agriculture, mining, and domestic work, the latter do not tend to die out, but to form a servile class. This is the case, not only in tropical countries where white men cannot form real colonies, working and rearing families with safety and efficiency, and where hard manual work, if done at all, must be done by "coloured men," but even in countries where white men can settle, as in parts of South Africa and of the southern portion of the United States.

As we entered these countries for trade, so we stay there for industrial exploitation, directing to our own profitable purposes the compulsory labour of the lower races. This is the root fact of Imperialism so far as it relates to the control of inferior races; when the latter are not killed out they are subjected by force to the ends of their white superiors.

With the abolition of the legal form of slavery the economic substance has not disappeared. It is no general question of how far the character of slavery adheres in all wage labour that I am pressing, but a statement that Imperialism rests upon and exists for the sake of "forced labour," i.e. labour which natives would not undertake save under direct or indirect personal compulsion issuing from white masters. . . .

The simplest form of this compulsion is that of employing armed force upon individual natives to "compel them to come in," as illustrated by the methods of the South Africa Chartered Company before 1897, which, when the chiefs failed to provide labour, sent out native police to "collect the labour." Save its illegal character, there is nothing to distinguish this from the *corvée* or legalized forced labour imposed on natives in Natal, or the Compulsory Labour Ordinance passed by the Gold Coast Legislature in December 1895, reviving the lapsed custom under which it was "obligatory on persons of the labouring class to give labour for public purposes on being called out by their chiefs or other native superiors," and authorizing the Government to compel native chiefs to furnish as many carriers as were needed. . . .

. . . The classical instance is that of the Congo Free State, where a "militia" levy was made upon the population, nominally for defence, but really for the State and Chartered Company service in the "rubber" and other industries. . . .

So far as "forced labour" is designed merely as a mode of revenue to the State, a system of "taxation in kind," it cannot be condemned as essentially unjust or oppressive, however liable it may be to abuses in practice. All taxation is "forced labour," whether the tax be levied in money, in goods, or in service. When such "forced labour" is confined to the needs of a well-ordered government, and is fairly and considerately administered, it involves no particular oppression. Such "servitude" as it involves is concealed under every form of government. . . .

So far as Imperialism seeks to justify itself by sane civilization of lower races, it will endeavour to raise their industrial and moral status on their own lands, preserving as far as possible the continuity of the old tribal life and institutions, protecting them against the force and deceit of prospectors, labour touts, and other persons who seek to take their land and entice away their labour. If under the gradual teaching of industrial arts and the general educational influences of a white protectorate many of the old political, social, and religious institutions decay, that decay will be a natural wholesome process, and will be attended by the growth of new forms, not forced upon them, but growing out of the old forms and conforming to laws of natural growth in order to adapt native life to a changed environment.

But so long as the private, short-sighted, business interests of white farmers or white mine-owners are permitted, either by action taken on their own account or through pressure on a colonial or Imperial Government, to invade the lands of "lower peoples," and transfer to their private profitable purposes the land or labour, the first law of "sane" Imperialism is violated, and the phrases about teaching "the dignity of labour" and raising races of "children" to manhood, whether used by directors of mining companies or by statesmen in the House of Commons, are little better than wanton exhibitions of hypocrisy. They are based on a falsification of the facts, and a perversion of the motives which actually direct the policy.

EDMUND MOREL

From Affairs of West Africa

1902

Edmund D. Morel (1873–1924) was a British journalist, born in France, who specialized in European trade with West Africa. When he published the book Affairs of West Africa, *he was a member of the West African Section of the Liverpool Chamber of Commerce and a vocal advocate of British merchants. He became increasingly involved in humanitarian initiatives against labor exploitation and monopolistic trade practices by European regimes in Africa, particularly in Congo. In 1904, he became the founding secretary of the Congo Reform Association, which led the international humanitarian campaign for the reform of the Congo Free State. In this excerpt, Morel uses the term "West Africa" to identify a vast region that includes the Congo Free State and also the term "Domaine Privé" to refer to all of the lands of Congo that Leopold II arrogated by decree. He also refers to Leopold's support for and investment in concessionaire companies that gathered ivory and rubber within this territory. According to Morel, what is the fundamental problem facing the Congolese peoples? How should their welfare be ensured through reform?*

What are we in West Africa for? What do we hope to do there? What object took us there? What main purpose keeps us there? The answer is not for a moment in doubt. Commerce took us to West Africa; commerce keeps and will keep us in West Africa. . . . As in every other part of the world, commerce in West Africa is the outcome of supply and demand. There is a demand for the products of West Africa on the markets of the world, and there is a demand in West Africa for the products of European industrialism. . . .

. . . Commerce is the greatest civilising agent. The steps upward in the ethical development of the human race have been synonymous with the spread of commercial relations, and the creation of the means and

Edmund D. Morel, *Affairs of West Africa* (London: William Heinemann, 1902), 21–22, 328–31, 333–34, 341–42, 351–52.

measures whereby their promotion has been successively extended. The most backward peoples to-day are, generally speaking, those whose secluded habitat renders their commercial transactions with the outside world scanty and precarious. In these days, when the noble meaning which attaches to "philanthropy" and "civilisation" is made the cloak to cover in West Africa so much that is vile, the excuse both sincerely and hypocritically given to explain away so much that is in painful contradiction, one needs, perhaps, to be reminded that such commonplace things as commerce and improved means of communication will do more to benefit the native than any number of attempts to impose laws and institutions unfamiliar to him, by violent even if well-meaning measures of so-called reform. . . .

. . . The vast territories of the *Domaine Privé* have for eleven years been absolutely closed to legitimate private enterprise. Trade, which in Central Africa means the exchange of European merchandise for raw products, does not exist therein. The native living within these territories has been deprived by Royal Decree of his rights as a land-owner. Property held for centuries by well-defined native laws, vested in particular families and tribes, has been appropriated without consulting the interested parties, let alone compensating them. With the deprivation of his land the native has been dispossessed of the fruits thereof; the rubber growing so luxuriously in his forests he may (by decree) only gather for the State—we will see presently how the "may" becomes "must"; the ivory stacked about his villages is no longer his, but another's; the elephants which roam about his country and damage his plantations he can incur the physical peril of destroying, but may not reap the reward to which he is thereby entitled, for the tusks of the slain beast do not, according to Royal Decree, belong to him. Since he cannot dispose of his produce, which is his wealth and also his currency; since he has lost his rights in his own land . . . he is no longer a free agent, but has become *de facto* a serf. . . .

The *Domaine Privé* is "worked" in two ways. The country is vaguely divided into districts, and the business of the *Commissaires* of districts, and their agents and sub-agents, is to collect *impôis de nature*, the taxes in kind, which the king levies. There is no limit to this taxation. The *Commissaires* are told to "devote all their energies to the harvesting of rubber," but at the same time to proceed "*as far as possible* by persuasion rather than force." The purport of the instructions may be briefly summed up thus: "Obtain all the rubber and ivory you can; your future advancement depends upon your energy." Of course, this *régime* in a country like Africa, where the native is not obliged to "work" in order to live, would be so much beating of the air, if force were not used to give it practical effect. King Leopold understood that well enough, and, to use the expression of a French Colonial writer of repute—M. Pierre Mille—"the basis of the king's economic policy has been the formation of an army sufficiently strong to force the natives to pay the rubber and ivory tax." A large army, chiefly recruited from the Bangalas and Batetlas—both cannibal tribes—was raised, and when not engaged in rebelling against its officers, it has proved only too well its value.

Side by side with the enforcement of the *impôts de nature*, King Leopold bethought him of another scheme whereby to increase his revenue, and, at the same time, to throw dust in the eyes of European public opinion, by professing to sanction private enterprise in the *Domaine Privé*. His Majesty took to farming out portions of his domain to certain financiers with whom it suited him to keep on good terms. "Companies" were formed, in which the State retained a half interest. These companies are supposed to obtain the rubber and ivory they ship home in such large quantities by barter; but as more often than not the king's officials and the companies' agents are the same persons, and as the companies have the assistance of the *Force Publique* (or permission to raise their own forces) to facilitate their commercial operations, we may judge of the amount of legitimate barter trade which is carried on. . . .

The performances of [a] particular offshoot of King Leopold's *Domaine Privé* [the Company of Antwerp for Trade in Congo] have been worthy of the regenerating nature of the Congo State rule. In 1900, one or two of its agents confessed to killing, by order, 150 natives, cutting off 60 hands, crucifying women and children, and impaling the sexual remains of slaughtered males on the stockade of the villages whose inhabitants were slow in gathering rubber! . . .

The cutting-off of hands item is a constantly recurring charge. I have in my possession at the present moment a photograph from the Upper Congo of three natives, a woman and two boys; the woman and one of the boys have their right hands severed at the wrist, the other boy has both hands severed. The correspondent who sent it me—and whom I know to be an honourable man—saw the victims himself, and was satisfied that soldiers of the State were the culprits. . . .

The edicts of the Congo State administration, coupled with certain material facts as to which there can be no dispute, show the main factors, if one may say so, of the system of African tropical development, which it has instituted, to be these:

(1) Alienation of native ownership in land.
(2) Monopoly over the products of the soil.

(3) Natives forbidden to collect those products for any one but the State, or the subsidiary trusts (*Domaine Privé* companies, if that appellation be preferred) created by the State, and in whose profits the State shares, generally to the extent of 50 per cent.

(4) Natives compelled to bring in rubber and ivory, and also recruits for the native army (and for labour in the cocoa and coffee plantations), to the State as tribute, and to supply the subsidiary trusts with rubber and ivory.

(5) The existence of a regular army of fifteen thousand men armed with Albini rifles, and an unnamed number of irregulars to enforce the rubber and ivory tribute and to "facilitate the operations" of the subsidiary trusts.

(6) White officials in receipt of instructions to devote all their energies to the exploitation of rubber and ivory; in plain words, to get as much rubber and ivory out of their respective districts as they possibly can.

(7) The financial existence of the State dependent upon the rubber and ivory tribute, and upon the profits it derives from its share in the subsidiary trusts.

When on the one side you have the factors already enumerated, and on the other a primitive and—in the face of coercion backed by rifles of precision—helpless population, common sense asserts that gross oppression, violence, and every form of tyranny and outrage must be the infallible outcome of such a system; and it is that *system* which the Powers are morally bound to put a stop to, seeing that it is they who are morally responsible for its existence.

This accursed *Domaine Privé*, and all the evils it has brought with it, cannot last for ever. Like all such "negations of God" it will perish. But what will remain behind for Europe, when the Congo State has passed away, to deal with? A vast region, peopled by fierce Bantu races, with an undying hatred of the white implanted in their breasts; a great army of cannibal levies, drilled in the science of forest warfare, perfected in the usage of modern weapons of destruction—savages whose one lesson learned from contact with European "civilisation" has been improvement in the art of killing their neighbours; disciplined in the science of slaughter; eager to seize upon the first opportunity which presents itself of turning their weapons against their temporary masters; rendered more desperate, more dangerous, more debased than before the advent of King Leopold's rubber collectors, who, by way of regeneration, have grafted upon the native's failings, born of ignorance, the worst vices of the Africanised civilisation of modern Europe—cupidity, hypocrisy, cruelty, and lust.

In their own most obvious interests, for the sake of humanity and right, in the name of enlightened statesmanship and political common sense, the Powers cannot allow the disease introduced into West and Central Africa by King Leopold of Belgium to be farther extended. Nor do their responsibilities end there. The source of the disease must be dealt with. The canker must be rooted out and cast upon the dunghill. The Congo State must be called to account for its crimes against civilisation; for its outrages upon humanity; for the unparalleled and irreparable mischief it has committed.

22

ROGER CASEMENT

Consular Report on the Congo Free State to the British Foreign Secretary

February 1904

Roger Casement (1864–1916), an Irishman who served as a British consular official, wrote this report on the basis of several months of travel in the Congo Free State and interviews with many Europeans and Congolese peoples in 1903. Much of this excerpt refers to the region and events covered by the Congolese oral histories in Documents 11–14 and the accounts by the Reverends John Murphy and E. V. Sjöblom and Governor-General Théophile Wahis (Documents 15–17). Throughout the report, Casement uses letters, or what appear to be initials, instead of the names of people and places. For example, the last item in this excerpt is a transcript of the testimony by a woman identified as "QQ." He did this to protect people from reprisals. It is noteworthy that Casement's investigation was largely guided by Protestant missionaries, who often provided transportation, translation services, and contacts among local peoples. The British government and humanitarians treated his findings as critical proof of the alleged brutality of the regime. The report inspired the creation of the Congo Reform Association, of which Casement was a founding member.

"Correspondence and Report from His Majesty's Consul at Boma respecting the Administration of the Independent State of the Congo," in *Accounts and Papers of the British Parliament*, vol. 62, cd. 1933 (1904), 42–47, 50–51, 72.

It also prompted Leopold II to dispatch his own commission of inquiry to investigate alleged abuses and atrocities in Congo in 1905.

With my arrival in the Lulongo [Lulonga] River, I was entering one of the most productive rubber districts of the Congo State, where the industry is said to be in a very flourishing condition. The Lulongo is formed by two great feeders—the Lopori and Maringa Rivers—which, after each a course of some 350 miles through a rich, forested country, well peopled by a tribe named Mongos, unite at Bassankusu [Basankusu], some 120 miles above where the Lulongo enters the Congo. The basins of these two rivers form the Concession known as the A.B.I.R., which has numerous stations, and a staff of fifty-eight Europeans engaged in exploiting the india-rubber industry, with head-quarters at Bassankusu. Two steamers belonging to the A.B.I.R. Company navigate the waterways of the Concession, taking up European goods and bringing down to Bassankusu the india-rubber, which is there transhipped on board a Government steamer which plies for this purpose between Coquilhatville and Bassankusu, a distance of probably 160 miles. The transport of all goods and agents of the A.B.I.R. Company, immediately these quit the Concession, is carried on exclusively by the steamers of the Congo Government, the freight and passage-money obtained being reckoned as part of the public revenue. I have no actual figures giving the annual output of india-rubber from the A.B.I.R. Concession, but it is unquestionably large, and may, in the case of a prosperous year, reach from 600 to 800 tons. The quality of the A.B.I.R. rubber is excellent, and it commands generally a high price on the European market, so that the value of its annual yield may probably be estimated at not less than 150,000. The merchandise used by the Company consists of the usual class of Central African barter goods—cotton cloths of different quality, Sheffield cutlery, matchets [machetes], beads, and salt. The latter is keenly sought by the natives of all the interior of Africa. There is also a considerable import by the A.B.I.R. Company, I believe, of cap-guns, which are chiefly used in arming the sentinels—termed "forest guards"—who, in considerable numbers, are quartered on the native villages throughout the Concession to see that the picked men of each town bring in, with regularity, the fixed quantity of pure rubber required of them every fortnight. . . .

The right of the various Concession Companies operating within the Congo State to employ armed men—whether these bear rifles or cap-guns—is regulated by Government enactments, which confer on these commercial Societies what are termed officially "rights of police" ("droits de police"). A Circular of the Governor-General dealing with this question, dated the 20th October, 1900, points out the limits within which this right may be exercised. Prior to the issue of this Circular . . . , the various Concession Companies would appear to have engaged in military operations on a somewhat extensive scale, and to have made war upon the natives on their own account. . . . That the extensive use of armed men in the pay of the so-called Trading Societies, or in the service of the Government, as a means to enforce the compliance with demands for india-rubber, had been very general up to a recent date, is not denied by any one I met on the Upper Congo.

In a conversation with a gentleman of experience on this question, our remarks turned upon the condition of the natives. He produced a disused diary, and in it, I found and copied the following entry:—

> M. P. called on us to get out of the rain, and in conversation with M. Q. in presence of myself and R., said: "The only way to get rubber is to fight for it. The natives are paid 35 centimes per kilog., it is claimed, but that includes a large profit on the cloth; the amount of rubber is controlled by the number of guns, and not the number of bales of cloth. The S.A.B. on the Bussira [Busira], with 150 guns, get only 10 tons (rubber) a-month; we, the State, at Momboyo, with 130 guns, get 13 tons per month." "So you count by guns?" I asked him. "Partout [Everywhere]," M. P. said, "Each time the corporal goes out to get rubber cartridges are given to him. He must bring back all not used; and for every one used, he must bring back a right hand." M. P. told me that sometimes they shot a cartridge at an animal in hunting; they then cut off a hand from a living man. As to the extent to which this is carried on, he informed me that in six months they, the State, on the Momboyo River, had used 6,000 cartridges, which means that 6,000 people are killed or mutilated. It means more than 6,000, for the people have told me repeatedly that the soldiers kill children with the butt of their guns.

In conversation upon this entry, I was told that the M. P. referred to was an officer in the Government service, who, at the date in question, had come down from the Momboyo River (a tributary of the great Ruki River, and forming a part, I believe, of the "Domaine de la Couronne") invalided, on his way home. He had come down in very bad health. He stated then that he was going home, not to return to the Congo, but he died, only a little way further down the river, very soon afterwards. . . .

The region drained by the Lulongo being of great fertility has, in the past, maintained a large population. In the days prior to the establishments of civilized rule in the interior of Africa, this river offered a constant source of supply to the slave markets of the Upper Congo. The towns around the lower Lulongo River raided the interior tribes, whose prolific humanity provided not only servitors, but human meat for those stronger than themselves. Cannibalism had gone hand in hand with slave raiding, and it was no uncommon spectacle to see gangs of human beings being conveyed for exposure and sale in the local markets. I had in the past, when travelling on the Lulongo River, more than once viewed such a scene. On one occasion a woman was killed in the village I was passing through, and her head and other portions of her were brought and offered for sale to some of the crew of the steamer I was on. Sights of this description are to-day impossible in any part of the country I traversed, and the full credit for their suppression must be given to the authorities of the Congo Government. It is, perhaps, to be regretted that in its efforts to suppress such barbarous practices the Congo Government should have had to rely upon, often, very savage agencies wherewith to combat savagery. The troops employed in punitive measures were — and often are — themselves savages, only removed by outward garb from those they are sent to punish. Moreover, the measures employed to obtain recruits for the public service were themselves often but little removed from the malpractices that service was designed to suppress. The following copy of an order of Government workmen drawn up by a former Commissaire of the Equator District, and having reference to the Maringa affluent of the Lulongo River indicates that the Congo Government itself did not hesitate some years ago to purchase slaves (required as soldiers or workmen), who could only be obtained for sale by the most deplorable means: —

Le Chef Ngulu de Wangata est envoyé dans la Maringa, pour m'y acheter des esclaves. Prière à MM. les agents de l'A.B.I.R. de bien vouloir me signaler les méfaits que celui-ci pourrait commettre en route. [Chief Ngulu from Wangata was sent to Maringa to buy slaves for me. I pray, Sirs, agents of the A.B.I.R., that you would inform me of any misdeeds that he might commit along the way.]

Le Capitaine-Commandant,

[Signed] SARRAZYN

Colquilhatville [Coquilhatville], *le* 1*er Mai*, 1896.

This document was shown to me during the course of my journey. The officer who issued this direction was, I was informed, for a considerable period chief executive authority of the district; and I heard him frequently spoken of by the natives who referred to him by the sobriquet he had earned in the district, "Widjima," or "Darkness." . . .

The Concession Companies, I believe, account for the armed men in their service on the ground that their factories and agents must be protected against the possible violence of the rude forest dwellers with whom they deal; but this legitimate need for safeguarding European establishments does not suffice to account for the presence, far from those establishments, of large numbers of armed men quartered throughout the native villages, and who exercise upon their surroundings an influence far from protective. The explanation offered me of this state of things was that, as the "impositions" laid upon the natives were regulated by law, and were calculated on the scale of public labour the Government had a right to require of the people, the collection of these "impositions" had to be strictly enforced. When I pointed out that the profit of this system was not reaped by the Government, but by a commercial Company, and figured in the public returns of that Company's affairs, as well as in the official Government statistics, as the outcome of commercial dealings with the natives, I was informed that the "impositions" were in reality trade, "for, as you observe, we pay the natives for the produce they bring in." "But," I observed, "you told me just now that these products did not belong to the natives, but to you, the Concessionnaire, who owned the soil; how, then, do you buy from them what is already yours?" "We do not buy the india-rubber. What we pay to the native is a remuneration for his labour in collecting our produce on our land, and bringing it to us."

Since it was thus to the labour of the native alone that the profits of the Company were attributed, I inquired whether he was not protected by contract with his employer; but I was here referred back to the statement that the native performed these services as a public duty required of him by his Government. He was not a contracted labourer at all, but a free man, dwelling in his own home, and was simply acquitting himself of an "imposition" laid upon him by the Government, "of which we are but the collectors by right of our Concession." "Your Concession, then, implies," I said, "that you have been conceded not only a certain area of land, but also the people dwelling on that land." This, however, was not accepted either, and I was assured that the people were absolutely free, and owed no service to any one but to the Government of the country. But there was no explanation offered to me that was not at once contradicted by the next. One said it was a tax, an obligatory burden laid upon the people, such as all Governments have the undoubted right of imposing; but this failed to explain how, if a tax, it came to be collected by the agents of a trading firm, and figured as the outcome of their trade dealings with the people, still less, how, if it were a tax, it could be justly imposed every week or fortnight in the year, instead of once, or at most, twice a year. . . .

. . . The summing up of the situation by the majority of those with whom I sought to discuss it was that, in fact, it was forced labour conceived in the true interest of the native, who, if not controlled in this way, would spend his days in idleness, unprofitable to himself and the general community. The collection of the products of the soil by the more benevolent methods adopted by the Trading Companies was, in any case, preferable to those the Congo Government would itself employ to compel obedience to this law, and therefore if I saw women and children seized as hostages and kept in detention until rubber or other things were brought in, it was better that this should be done by the cap-gun of the "forest guard" than by the Albini armed soldiers of the Government who, if once impelled into a district, would overturn the entire country side.

No more satisfactory explanation than this outline was anywhere offered me of what I saw in the A.B.I.R. and Lulanga districts. . . .

At a village I touched at up the Lulonga River, a small collection of dwellings named Z*, the people complained that there was no rubber left in their district, and yet that the La [Lulonga] Company required of them each fortnight a fixed quantity they could not supply. Three forest guards of that Company were quartered, it was said, in this village, one of whom I found on duty, the two others, he informed me, having gone to Mampoko to convoy the fortnight's rubber. No livestock of any kind could be seen or purchased in this town, which had only a few years ago been a large and populous community, filled with people and well stocked with sheep, goats, ducks, and fowls. Although I walked through most of it, I could only count ten men with their families. There were said to be others in the part of the town I did not visit, but the entire community I saw were living in wretched houses and in most visible distress. Three months previously (in May, I believe), they said a Government force, commanded by a white man, had occupied their town owing to their failure to send in to the Mampoko head-quarters of the La [Lulonga] Company a regular supply of india-rubber, and two men, whose names were given, had been killed by the soldiers at that time.

As Z* lies upon the main stream of the [Lulonga] River, and is often touched at by passing steamers, I chose for the next inspection a town lying somewhat off this beaten track, where my coming would be quite unexpected. Steaming up a small tributary of the [Lulonga], I arrived, unpreceded by any rumour of my coming, at the village of A**. In an open shed I found two sentries of the La [Lulonga] Company guarding fifteen native women, five of whom had infants at the breast, and three of whom were about to become mothers. The chief of these sentries, a man called S— who was bearing a double-barrelled shot-gun, for which he had a belt of cartridges—at once volunteered an explanation of the reason for these women's detention. Four of them, he said, were hostages who were being held to insure the peaceful settlement of a dispute between two neighbouring towns, which had already cost the life of a man. His employer, the agent of the La [Lulonga] Company at B** near by, he said, had ordered these women to be seized and kept until the Chief of the offending town to which they belonged should come in to talk over the palaver. The sentry pointed out that this was evidently a much better way to settle such troubles between native towns than to leave them to be fought out among the people themselves.

The remaining eleven women, whom he indicated, he said he had caught and was detaining as prisoners to compel their husbands to bring in the right amount of india-rubber required of them on next market day. When I asked if it was a woman's work to collect india-rubber, he said, "No, that, of course, it was man's work." "Then why do you catch the women and not the men?" I asked. "Don't you see," was the answer, "if I caught and kept the men, who would work the rubber? But if I catch their wives, the husbands are anxious to have them home again, and so the rubber is brought in quickly and quite up to the mark." When I asked what would become of these women if their husbands failed to bring in the right quantity of rubber on the next market day, he said at once that then they would be kept there until their husbands had redeemed them. Their food, he explained, he made the Chief of A** provide, and he himself saw it given to them daily. They came from more than one village of the neighbourhood, he said, mostly from the Ngombi or inland country, where he often had to catch women to insure the rubber being brought in in sufficient quantity. It was an institution, he explained, that served well and saved much trouble. When his master came each fortnight to A** to take away the rubber so collected, if it was found to be sufficient, the women were released and allowed to return with their husbands, but if not sufficient they would undergo continued detention. The sentry's statements were clear and explicit, as were equally those of several of the villagers with whom I spoke. The sentry further explained, in answer to my inquiry, that he caught women in this way by direction of his employers. That it was a custom generally adopted and found to work well; that the people were very lazy, and that this was much the simplest way of making them do what was required of them. When asked if he had any use for his shot-gun, he answered that it had been given him by the white man "to frighten people and make them bring in rubber," but that he had never otherwise used it. I found that the two sentries at A** were complete masters of the town. Everything

I needed in the way of food or firewood they at once ordered the men of the town to bring me. One of them, gun over shoulder, marched a procession of men—the Chief of the village at their head—down to the water side, each carrying a bundle of firewood for my steamer. A few chickens which were brought were only purchased through their intermediary, the native owner in each case handing the fowl over to the sentry, who then brought it on board, bargained for it, and took the price agreed upon. When, in the evening, the Chief of the village was invited to come and talk to me, he came in evident fear of the sentries seeing him or overhearing his remarks, and the leader, S, finding him talking to me, peremptorily broke into the conversation and himself answered each question put to the Chief. When I asked this latter if he and his townsmen did not catch fish in the C** River, in which we learned there was much, the sentry, intervening, said it was not the business of these people to catch fish—"they have no time for that, they have got to get the rubber I tell them to." . . .

On the . . . September a man named T came to see me. He had been very badly wounded in the thigh, and walked with difficulty. He stated that a sentry of the A.B.I.R., a man named U, had shot him, as I saw; and at the same time had killed V, a friend. The sentries had come to arrest the Chief of H** on account of meat, which was short for the white man—not the present white man, but another—and his people had gathered around the Chief to protect him. An inquiry I gathered had been held by a Law Officer into this and other outrages committed the previous year, and as a result the sentry U had been removed from the district. T went on to say to me that this sentry was now back in the country at large, and a free man. When I asked him if he himself had not been compensated for the injuries entailing partial disablement he had received, he said: "Four months ago I was arrested for not having got meat, and was kept one and a half months in prison on that account. U, who killed V, and shot me here in the thigh, is a free man, as all men know; but I, who am wounded, have to hunt meat."

This statement I found on fuller inquiry in other quarters was confirmed; and it became apparent that while the murderer was at large, one of those he had seriously injured, and almost incapacitated, was still required to hunt game, and paid for his failure by imprisonment. On further inquiry, I gathered that this occasion was the only one locally known when a qualified Law Officer had ever visited the Lopori, although charges from that region involving very grave accusations had, on several occasions, been preferred. There being no Magistrate resident in the whole of the A.B.I.R. Concession, inquiries, unless conducted by the agents of the A.B.I.R. themselves, have to be investigated at Coquilhat-ville—distant fully 270 miles from Bongandanga, and over 400 miles from some parts of the Concession.

It is true an officer of the Congo Executive is deputed to exercise a qualified surveillance within this Concession; but he is not a qualified Magistrate or legally empowered to act as such.

The occupant of this post is a military officer of inferior rank, who is quartered, with a force of soldiers, near to Basankusu, the chief station of the A.B.I.R. Company.

This officer, when he enters the A.B.I.R. territory, is accompanied by soldiers, and his actions would appear to be generally confined to measures of a punitive kind, the necessity for such measures being that which almost everywhere applies—namely, a refusal of or falling off in the supplies of india-rubber.

At the date of my visit to the Lopori he was engaged in a journey, not unconnected with fighting, to the Maringa River. His independence is not complete, nor is his disassociation from the A.B.I.R. Company's agencies as marked as, in view of the circumstances attending the collection of rubber, it should be.

His journeys up the two great rivers, the Maringa and Lopori, which drain the A.B.I.R. territory, are made on the steamers of that Company, and he is, to all intents, a guest of the Company's agents.

The supervision of this officer extends also over the course of the [Lulonga] river, outside the A.B.I.R. Concession, and he it was who had occupied the town of Z* on an occasion some months before my visit, when two native men had been killed.

The Commissaire-Général of the Equator District has also, at recent periods, visited the A.B.I.R. Concession, but this officer, although the Chief of the Executive and the President of the Territorial Court of the entire district, came as a visitor to the A.B.I.R. stations and as [a] guest on the steamer of that Company.

No steamer belonging to the Congo Government regularly ascends either the Lopori or Maringa rivers, and the conveyance of mails from the A.B.I.R. territory depends, for steamer transport, on the two vessels of that Company. . . .

QQ* Statement

I was born at KK*. After my father died my mother and I went to LL*. When we returned to KK* soon after that PQ came to fight with us because of rubber. KK* did not want to take rubber to the white man.

We and our mothers ran away very far into the bush. The Bula Matadi soldiers were very strong and they fought hard, one soldier was killed, and they killed one KK* man. Then the white man said let us go home, and they went home, and then we, too, came out of the bush. This was the first fight. After that another fighting took place. I, my mother, grandmother, and my sister, we ran away into the bush. The soldiers came and fought us, and left the town and followed us into the bush. When the soldiers came into the bush near us they were calling my mother by name, and I was going to answer, but my mother put her hand to my mouth to stop me. Then they went to another side, and then we left that place and went to another. When they called my mother, if she had not stopped me from answering, we would all have been killed then. A great number of our people were killed by the soldiers. The friends who were left buried the dead bodies, and there was very much weeping. After that there was not any fighting for some time. Then the soldiers came again to fight with us, and we ran into the bush, but they really came to fight with MM*. They killed a lot of MM* people, and then one soldier came out to KK* and the KK* people killed him with a spear. And when the other soldiers heard that their friend was killed they came in a large number and followed us into the bush. Then the soldiers fired a gun, and some people were killed. After that they saw a little bit of my mother's head, and the soldiers ran quickly towards the place where we were and caught my grandmother, my mother, my sister, and another little one, younger than us. Several of the soldiers argued about my mother, because each wanted her for a wife, so they finally decided to kill her. They killed her with a gun—they shot her through the stomach—and she fell, and when I saw that I cried very much, because they killed my mother and grandmother, and I was left alone. My mother was near to the time of her confinement at that time. And they killed my grandmother too, and I saw it all done. They took hold of my sister and asked where her older sister was, and she said; "She has just run away." They said, "Call her." She called me, but I was too frightened and would not answer, and I ran and went away and came out at another place, and I could not speak much because my throat was very sore. I saw a little bit kwanga [bread made from cassava] lying on the ground and I picked it up to eat. At that place there used to be a lot of people, but when I got there there were none. My sister was taken to P*, and I was at this place alone. One day I saw a man coming from the back country. He was going to kill me, but afterwards he took me to a place where there were people, and there I saw my step-father. He asked to buy me from this man, but the man would not let him. He said, "She is my slave now; I found her." One day the men went out fishing, and when I looked I saw the soldiers coming, so I ran away, but a string caught my foot and I fell, and a soldier named NNN caught me. He handed me over to another soldier, and as we went we saw some Q* people fishing, and the soldiers took a lot of fish from them and a Q* woman, and we went to P*, and they took me to the white man.

(Signed)   QQ.

Signed by QQ before me,
    (Signed)   ROGER CASEMENT
              His Britannic Majesty's Consul.

23

Atrocity Photograph of Epondo

ca. 1903

This photograph of the young man Epondo was probably taken by Daniel Jacob Danielson (1871–1916), a member of the Congo Balolo Mission who captained the vessel in which Casement conducted his consular investigation of the Congo Free State in 1903. According to Casement, Epondo testified that a state soldier cut off his hand, which supported humanitarian allegations that soldiers were mutilating Congolese people to provide an accounting of their spent rifle cartridges. Representatives of the Belgian regime asserted that Epondo informed them that his hand had been bitten off by a wild boar (see Document 25). This atrocity photograph typifies the images that British humanitarians used to great effect in lantern slide lectures to mobilize protest in Britain and the United States against the Congo Free State. The controversy over the cause of Epondo's mutilation demonstrates how even the validity of photographic evidence was contested by the state and its critics. How might a person in the early twentieth century have viewed this photograph in ways different from the ways in which we view it today? How does the meaning of this or any atrocity photograph depend on the narrative that accompanies it?

Samuel Clemens, *King Leopold's Soliloquy: A Defense of His Congo Rule* (Boston: P. R. Warren, 1905), plate opposite p. 38.

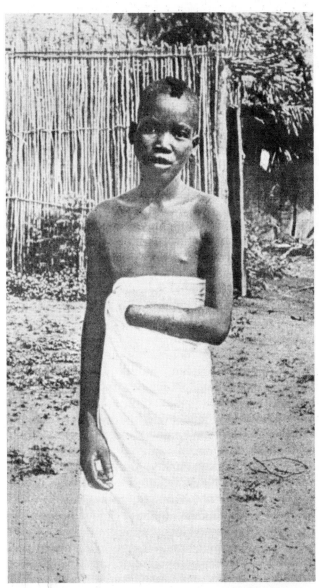

A child mutilated by Congo soldiery, Epondo, illustration from "King Leopold's Rule in Africa," 1905 (b/w photo) / Morel, Edmund Dene (1873–1924) / NEW YORK PUBLIC LIBRARY / New York Public Library, USA/Bridgeman Images.

24

PUNCH

In the Rubber Coils
November 28, 1906

This iconic representation of the Congo Free State appeared in one of the most popular periodicals in Great Britain. The cartoon portrays a huge snake with the head of Leopold II attacking a Congolese man, as a woman, with a child in her arms, flees. In the background, what appear to be pterodactyls fly across the sky. The image lends itself to a variety of symbolic interpretations. How do you interpret the historical significance and message of the cartoon? How would you compare its power with that of the photograph of Epondo (Document 23) as humanitarian texts?

"In the Rubber Coils," *Punch*, November 28, 1906, 389.

IN THE RUBBER COILS.

Scene—*The Congo "Free" State.*

111

25

The Congo: A Report of the Commission of Enquiry Appointed by the Congo Free State Government

October 31, 1905

*Roger Casement's 1904 consular report (Document 22) prompted Leo-
pold II to appoint his own commission of inquiry to investigate alleged
abuses in Congo. The president of the commission was Edmond Janssens,
attorney general of the supreme court of Belgium. He was joined by Giacomo Nisco, an Italian magistrate of long experience in Congo who later
presided over the court of appeals at Boma, and E. de Schumacher, a member of the Swiss Council of State and head of the Department of Justice
in the Swiss canton of Lucerne. This three-man commission traveled in
Congo between October 1904 and February 1905 as far as Stanley Falls,
hearing hundreds of testimonies by Congolese peoples and Europeans. Protestant missionaries were initially suspicious of the commission, but nonetheless encouraged the Congolese to testify. The commission's final report,
published in October 1905, validates many of Casement's charges, though
it refutes some, such as the state's responsibility for the mutilation of Epondo
(see Document 23). It also asserts that the Congo Free State deserved
praise for improving the conditions of most Congolese. Despite this positive, general assessment of the regime, humanitarians embraced the commission's report for its critical findings. How do this report and Casement's
report describe and explain abuses in Congo in different and similar ways?*

To the Secretary of State of the Congo Free State.

MR. SECRETARY OF STATE:

In obedience to the instructions contained in Article 5 of the Decree
of July 23, 1904, we have the honour to submit to you a Report upon the
results of the enquiry that we conducted in the Congo.

---

*The Congo: A Report of the Commission of Enquiry Appointed by the Congo Free State Gov-
ernment* (New York: G. P. Putnam's Sons, 1906), 1–2, 9–11, 26–29, 31, 33, 36, 66–69, 87,
90–91, 96–103, 163–67.

We had for our mission to "See if, in certain parts of the territory, the natives were subjected to ill treatment either by private individuals or by State Agents, to point out practical means of betterment and to formulate, in case the enquiry reveals such abuses, suggestions as to the best means of putting an end to the same, having in view the welfare of the inhabitants and the good government of the territories."

To aid in accomplishing this, the powers bestowed upon the State Attorney were conferred upon us. In accordance with the first Article of the Decree referred to above, we were to conduct this enquiry in conformity with the instructions of the Secretary of State. In your dispatch of Sept. 5, 1904, you informed us that "The Government had no other instructions to give the Commission than to devote all its efforts to the complete and entire discovery of the truth. It intends to leave the Commission, with this in view, its complete liberty, its individuality, and its initiative. The Government will depart from this principle of non-intervention in one respect only, that is, to give to its officials and agents of all rank formal and explicit orders to give to the Commission assistance and cooperation without reserve in order to help it in the accomplishment of its task." . . .

Although we had as our mission the investigation of the ill-treatment by the agents of which the natives might complain, and to verify the evils, still we did not think we would be prohibited from pointing out, in passing, the good which attracted our attention. Let us say at once, while on the voyage to the Congo, the comparison between the former conditions, known by the reports of explorers, and the present conditions created an impression of surprise and admiration.

In these regions which twenty years ago were still plunged in the most frightful barbarism and which had been crossed by only a few whites at the cost of superhuman efforts, met at every moment by the arrows of hostile people; in these districts where the tribes decimated by the raids of Arabian slave dealers fought each other without cessation and without mercy, where one encountered at every step the markets of human flesh where the buyers designated on the body of the victim the part which they coveted; where the funerals of the village chiefs were celebrated by the hecatomb [sacrifice] of slaves whom they strangled and the wives and women who were buried alive—in this dark and mysterious continent the State has been constituted and organised with marvellous rapidity, introducing into the heart of Africa the benefits of civilisation.

Today security reigns in this territory. Most everywhere the white who has not intimated hostile intentions can journey without escort and without arms. The slave trade has disappeared, cannibalism has been practically suppressed, pushed back, or is in hiding and sacrifices of human beings are rare. The villages, which call to mind our attractive sea-side towns, are numerous along the banks of the great river, and the two terminals of the Lower Congo Railway, Matadi, where the ocean steamers arrive, and Leopoldville, the great river-port with its activity and its warehouses, remind one of the industrial cities of Europe. The rural lines of Mayumbe, the railway of the Cataracts built in the most hilly regions, that of the Great Lakes, carried to the heart of the equatorial belt, the 24 steamers which float upon the Congo and its tributaries, the regular service of the postal communication, the telegraph lines that amount to 1200 kilometres, the hospitals established in the principal places, all of these things born of yesterday, give travellers the impression that they are in a country which has long enjoyed the blessings of European civilisation, and not in one which but a quarter of a century ago was totally unknown and savage. It makes one wonder what magic power or firm will, aided by heroic efforts, was able to so change a country in such a short time. . . .

Taxation

The greater part of the criticisms directed against the State is connected more or less directly with the question of taxation, and especially a tax payable in labour, the only one which affects the native.

This is without doubt the most important and the most complex question and upon the solution of this problem depends the solution of most of the others. . . .

JUSTIFICATION OF LABOUR TAXATION

All production, all commerce, all life in the Congo is only possible and will only endure by the aid of native labour. The white man, if he can become acclimated, can only with difficulty become able to endure the hard labour of the farmer and of the workman, and that too in a few favourable localities. On the other hand, the native by atavism and because of the conditions of the country has, in general, no predilection for work. He does only what is absolutely necessary for his subsistence. The fertility of the soil, the breadth of territory, the small amount of labour which cultivation demands, the clemency of the climate, all reduce to a minimum the sum total of necessary efforts; a few branches and some leaves suffice to shelter him; he wears no clothing, or practically none; fishing, hunting, and some crude farming give him easily the little nourishment which he needs; his energy is only stimulated by the desire to procure weapons, ornaments, or a wife; but, the desire once satisfied, there is nothing to be done but to exist. He is happy in his idleness. One finds exceptions amongst the most advanced races, like those of Kasai who have more extensive wants to satisfy, and amongst peoples formerly under Arab rule. These have been during many generations obliged to work and have acquired that habit; but as a general rule the natives desire nothing more than to be left with their ancient existence; no desire can attract them to a labour of any consequence, or of a fixed duration. . . .

Now the only means at the disposal of the State by which the native can be made to work is the imposition of a tax in labour; and it is precisely in view of the necessity of assuring to the State the indispensable labour of native hands that a tax in labour is justifiable in the Congo. This tax, besides, takes the place with the population of those restraining influences which, in civilised countries, are imposed by the conditions of life.

The principle by virtue of which the State demands of its citizens, in the public interests, not only a contribution in the shape of money or products, but also personal service—individual labour, is admitted by European codes. . . .

. . . It is in spite of himself that the native in the beginning must be induced to throw off his natural indolence and improve his condition. A law, therefore, which imposes upon the native light and regular work is the only means of giving him the incentive to work; while it is an economic law, it is at the same time a humanitarian law. It does not lose the last named character because it imposes some compulsion upon the native. To civilise a race means to modify its economic and social condition, its intellectual and moral status; it is to extirpate its ideas, customs and habits and substitute in the place of those of which we disapprove the ideas, habits and customs which are akin to ours; it is, in a word, to assume the education of a people. All education which concerns a child or an inferior race necessarily inflicts a curtailment of liberty. . . .

In a general way, it should be said, all that concerned the prescriptions and prestation [tax in kind] in relation to the natives, was until recent years left to the discretion of the agents. . . .

It happened, consequently, that very often the remuneration given to the natives was insufficient; sometimes even, they were paid in goods which had no value in that locality. The same uncertainty existed in regard to the means of compulsion when there was a necessity to use it in cases of non-payment of taxes. Agents on this point as on many others followed no rule. We shall point out in the course of this Report acts of violence more or less severe committed either towards individuals or against a people, where the use of force was the cause. . . .

COERCION

The dislike of the negro for all kinds of work; his especial aversion to the rubber gathering, because of the circumstances indicated, and differing from the labour discussed in the preceding chapters because the native has not been prepared for it by the customs of previous generations; finally the contact with the white, which, having existed for only a short time, has not created in him new wants which make him almost indifferent to the proffered remuneration; all of these circumstances have made compulsion necessary to induce the native to gather rubber.

Until recent years this coercion has been exercised in different ways, such as, the taking of hostages, the detention of chiefs and the institution of sentinels or bosses and the sending of armed expeditions.

Coercion, Properly So Called, Exercised by the Whites

In the absence of a specific law and precise instruction upon the subject, the agents charged with the exercise of coercion, applying the principle of solidarity which exists amongst those who are the subjects of the same chief, often trouble themselves but little to seek out the real culprit. The prestations were due from the village as a whole; when they were not forthcoming the chiefs were arrested and some of the inhabitants taken at random, often the women were held as hostages. This system had for its purpose the moral compulsion upon the delinquents to stimulate their efforts in order to liberate their chief or their wives. This proved efficacious and, perhaps, as we were often told, did not appear in the eyes of the natives, imbued with the idea of solidarity, so reprehensible as it would to us. But whatever one may think of the ideas of the natives, any procedure, such as the detention of the women as hostages, outrages our notion of justice too violently to be tolerated. The State has, for a long time, forbidden this practice, but has been unable to suppress it. Likewise the arrest of the chiefs, who are not always personally to blame, has the effect of diminishing their authority or even completely destroying it; especially when they are seen forced to servile labour.

The same may be said of the system by which the agents fix the length of the detention. From the statements of witnesses and the official documents that we saw, we found that this detention may have been continued, in certain cases, for several months.

Some have told us, it is true, that those under detention at the post are not badly treated nor compelled to perform excessive labour. They have also asserted that the lot of the women is less oppressive here than under the animal-like existence to which they are subjected in their own villages. Nevertheless, it is beyond question that the detention is often aggravated by conditions which attend it. We have been told that the places in which the prisoners were kept were sometimes in a bad condition, that they often lacked the necessities and that the mortality amongst them was very great.

Some chiefs of posts, assuming a right that never belonged to them[,] administer the lash to those who fail to furnish the complete imposts. Some have carried this to excess, as is shown by the record of their punishment by the courts.[1]

These abuses are certainly not unknown in the private domain. From a study of the documents placed at the disposal of the Commission or demanded by it, we became acquainted with the majority of the facts testified to by the Reverends Whitehead (Lukolela), Weeks (Monsembe), and Gilchrist (Lulonga).

Acts of violence have been committed in the region of Lake Leopold II, Bangala, Lake Tumba, in Uele and Aruwimi. But all witnesses confess that great improvements have taken place in recent times. Two Evangelical missionaries from the district of Lake Leopold II (the Crown Domain exploited by State agents), where the rule had been the object of very severe criticism by one of them, said to us: "according to what we have been told, everything is now going well in this region"; and the other said, that he had observed during a recent visit to this district, that the situation was good in comparison with what it had been before.

Unfortunately, the same does not seem to be true in those regions exploited by private companies. From an examination of documents regarding Mongala, and a careful enquiry made by the Commission in regard to the Abir [Anglo-Belgian India Rubber and Exploration Company] concession it appears that acts of the sort of which we are speaking, were very frequent in the territory controlled by these companies. At the different posts in the Abir which we visited, it was never denied that the imprisonment of women as hostages, the imposition of servile work on chiefs, the administration of the lash to delinquents and the abuse of authority by the black overseers were, as a rule, habitual.

---

[1] The blacks who are assigned to guard the prisoners occasionaily overstep their authority and become brutal. [All footnotes from the original document.]

Similar conditions have been reported to the Commission from Lulonga.

Most of these facts were unknown to the officials until a recent enquiry of a deputy revealed them, so that it is likely that the freedom from punishment was accountable for their continuance. . . .

Military Expeditions

State Expeditions

We shall not speak of the expeditions which had for their purpose the subjugation of the natives or the suppression of their revolutions. These operations were, in reality, acts of war with which we have nothing to do as our duties must not entrench upon the rights of the State.

Outside of this category there are military expeditions which are right and necessary to insure the maintenance of order or the respect for law, but such expeditions should not assume the character of war in which martial law takes the place of civil law; they are police operations in which the members, in doing everything that is requisite for the restoration of order, must act within legal bounds and respect the rights of the people.

It is the abusive military operations having a warlike nature, which we feel ought to be mentioned. They are frequently occasioned by the collection of imposts and the repression of offences. . . .

It often happens that the natives in order to avoid the payment of the imposts, especially the rubber tax, migrate either singly or as a mass and establish themselves in another region or even in another district. The detachment of troops is then sent to bring back the fugitives either by persuasion or after a combat. . . .

. . . The State can be expected to bring them back to their homes and villages and to impose upon them work, using only its right of coercion, and after having brought the contributors back to their homes it could subject them to imprisonment and enforced labour. But this reasoning is not sufficient to justify the use of arms against a population whose rebellion, if this term may be employed here, has been purely passive. . . .

Expeditions Sent Out by the Companies

The companies can never send out armed expeditions. They are permitted to have at each of their factories twenty-five Albini rifles, of which twenty are for the exclusive purpose of repelling attacks to which they may be subjected by the natives. The other five can be assigned, under special permission, to men detailed to escort the whites in the trips which they must make throughout the territory included within the concession. In addition to these improved weapons, muzzle-loading (flint-lock) guns can be entrusted to the black *capitas* [sentries] at isolated stations, who must be supplied with a permit to have arms. "These guns," says a circular of the Governor General, "can be taken out from the factories only singly. They cannot pass out of the hands of the commercial companies into the hands of groups more or less important nor be used by an offensive force." In spite of this formal interdiction, it has happened on several occasions that the commercial agents have made visits escorted by a number of men armed with Albini rifles in excess of the number permitted by the instructions. It has also happened that these visits have assumed the character of real military expeditions. In some cases armed bands have been sent into villages of natives without being accompanied by any whites. During these irregular operations the greatest abuses have been committed; men have been killed as well as women and children, often even when they were fleeing; others have been made prisoners and the wives taken as hostages. From the documents and judicial reports that have been examined by the Commission it appears that acts of this sort have taken place, notably in Mongala. In the Abir concession visited by the Commission, similar abuses were denounced by the missionaries of the Congo Balolo Mission as well as by the deputies and many native witnesses appeared to confirm these declarations. The deputies likewise reported armed expeditions undertaken by agents of the Lomami and the Kasai companies. More than that, the reports of the commercial agents as well as the many sentences passed by the courts prove beyond a doubt the existence of these reprehensible acts. The greater part of the whites now in prison in Boma are under punishment for crimes of this sort.

Many times the agents of the companies, who take part in these expeditions or who order them, thought they had the right to claim the "police authority" which is conferred upon them. But this error of interpretation is no longer admissible since the circular of the Governor General dated October 20, 1900, reminding the companies that the police authority is "never the right to carry on offensive military operations, to make war against the natives, but simply gives the authority to requisition, for the purpose of maintaining order or establishing it, the armed force that is in the concession or outside actually under the command of State officers."

The Government has, in fact, placed upon certain concessions a police force charged with the protection and supervision of the territory which is directly under the authority of the District Commissioner. The directors of the companies may summon them directly in case of extreme need.

From what we could see it seems that these troops are devoted to the directors and agents, who call upon them every time the pecuniary interests of the company are involved.

THE MUTILATIONS

It is chiefly in the course of the armed expeditions that the acts of mutilation took place to which several witnesses, and especially the Protestant missionaries, called the attention of the Commission.

At Lake Tumba, at Ikoko, the missionaries and several blacks told us that they saw, about 1895, in a canoe occupied by soldiers, a basket containing a dozen or twenty hands. Reverend Mr. Clark declared that at about the same time he saw in a canoe some hands fastened to a stick; they seemed to have been smoked. Both canoes were turned towards Bikoro. A native stated that these hands were shown to the chief of the Bikoro post and Mr. Clark reports that this same agent, now deceased, pointing to his dog said of him: "There is a cannibal dog, he eats hands that have been cut off."

The same missionary, Mrs. Clark and Mrs. Whitman told us that on several occasions they saw natives killed in the course of expeditions made by the State, from whom the right hand had been cut off. Mr. and Mrs. Clark, also a black witness, testified to having seen a little girl whose right hand had been cut off during an expedition and who died at the end of six months, notwithstanding the best medical care, and also a woman whose hand had been similarly amputated. These missionaries finally told us of a native named Mola who had lost both hands as the results of the brutalities inflicted by a soldier. This was confirmed by an investigation.[2]

Some black witnesses, coming from the district of Lake Leopold II, presented by Mr. Scrivener at Bolobo, declared that five or six years ago, their village being occupied by State troops after a battle, they saw seven genital organs taken from natives killed during the fight, and hung from a vine fastened to two sticks in front of the cabin occupied by the white.

The Commission also saw several mutilated persons.

At Coquilhatville we questioned the persons named Epondo and Ikabo. Epondo had his left hand cut off and Ikabo his right. [See Document 23.]

Mr. Clark at Ikobo brought before us Mputila from Yembe (Lake Tumba) who had lost his right hand.

---

[2]Mola had been captured by the soldiers. The cord with which he had been bound was too tight, causing gangrene to set in; he lost both hands.

Reverend Mr. Lower at Ikau brought before us Imponge from N'Songo, a boy apparently about fifteen years old, who had lost his right hand and left foot.

Reverend Mr. Harris at Baringa showed to us a person named Isekosu and the woman Boali, the former without his right hand and the latter without her right foot.

Epondo, repeating the story which he had told before, declared that he had lost his left hand as the result of a bite from a wild boar one day when he was hunting with his master.[3]

Imponge declares that, in his infancy, some sentries having attacked his village, his father fled carrying him in his arms. After a time his father dropped him in the brush so that he could run faster. A sentry saw him and cut off his right hand and left foot so as to take off the copper rings which he wore. This was confirmed by the father.

The woman Boali said that a *capita*, whose advances she had repulsed, shot her and thinking her dead, cut off her foot so as to be able to remove her anklet. . . .

From all of the cases verified by the Commission, it seems that the mutilation of the dead body is an ancient custom which does not have, in the eyes of the natives, the horrible character which it does in ours. The cutting off of certain parts of the body fills the native's desire for procuring either a trophy or simply a piece of evidence. Mutilation of enemies who were killed in the wars between natives of certain regions, is frequent. Even at the present time the black who wishes to show tangible proof of the death of another and can not show the dead body usually shows the hands and the feet of the same. . . .

One ought not to be astonished if the blacks enlisted in the constabulary have not been able to give up at once this ancient custom and if in order to furnish to their chiefs a proof of their bravery in war have occasionally carried home the trophy taken from the bodies of their enemies. It is more than likely that at the beginning of the occupation certain white agents have tolerated this barbarous custom or at least did not do all that was in their power to eradicate it. There result from this the regrettable acts pointed out to us and which we have confirmed: the mutilation of living persons whom the soldiers [or] the sentry had thought

---

[3]Without attaching any importance to the statements of Epondo, which have greatly varied during the course of the past two years, the Commission, relying upon its own verifications and upon the medical examination carefully made at Coquilhatville by Dr. Vedy, is convinced that Epondo actually lost his hand as the result of the bite of a wild animal. More than that, Reverend Mr. Weeks informed us that this was well known at Malele, where Epondo was born, as he had verified during a visit recently to that village.

dead. As to the mutilation of Imponge and the woman Boali, work of avaricious sentries, they had theft as a motive. Beyond these cases it then seems that the mutilations have never had the character of torture inflicted voluntarily and knowingly. However that may be, one point is beyond doubt, the white man has never inflicted or intended to inflict as a punishment for failure to make the prestation or for other causes, such mutilations upon living natives. Acts of this sort have not been reported by a single witness, nor have we discovered any, notwithstanding all our investigations. . . .

Justice

. . . Twenty centuries were necessary to create from Gaul, of the time of Cæsar, the France and Belgium of to-day and if our ancestors were, in the eyes of the conquering Romans, barbarians, one can, we think, say that they were civilised people in comparison with the inhabitants of the immense territory of the Free State at the moment of its constitution.

How should one expect that a code of laws as European as that of the Congo should not frequently meet in its application insurmountable obstacles? Hence arises a contradiction between the law and the fact; hence come those violations which the courts punish while granting to the offenders the benefits of extenuating circumstances.

The Court of Appeals, notably, has during the past years pronounced some decisions of remarkable severity, but it has always borne in mind the difficulties which have surrounded the Europeans. In order to live, to develop itself, the State found itself face to face with the necessity to exploit the natural wealth of the soil and the only available labour at its disposal was the native unused to work; the agents enervated by a terrible climate, always debilitating and often fatal, are isolated in the midst of a savage population; and the life of each day presents to them nothing but demoralising spectacles. They left Europe filled with respect for human life and they soon see in the barbarous circle into which they are transplanted, that this has no value. They were taught from infancy to love one's neighbour and they note amongst the savages around them an absolute ignorance of the sentiment called charity—the negro, in fact, can not realise that a thing can be done except from fear or hope of personal gain; they are witnesses in the villages of the miserable plight of the weak and the infirm upon whom the chiefs and head men always let fall the heaviest burdens; they see the women degraded to the condition of beasts of burden, labouring without interruption and performing every task. Those who have had this spectacle before their eyes understand, but do not condone, the ill-treatment, even the acts of brutality of the white man towards the native who leaves the post without food or towards the recalcitrant delinquent whom he accuses of indolence or ill-will, though the difficulties of the rubber harvest are seldom appreciated and the black man's aversion to labour is rarely understood. . . .

. . . The Free State, by the wonderful things it has accomplished in twenty years, gives the public the opportunity, we might almost say the right, to show itself exacting. In all events, it owes it to itself to introduce as soon as possible the reforms which we have cited, many of which are most urgent and can be accomplished without involving new expense. We have in view especially the large and liberal interpretation and application of the laws regarding the holding of real estate, the effective enforcement of the law limiting to forty hours per month the prestation of work, the suppression of the system of sentries, the permission for the *capitas* to carry arms, the revocation from the commercial companies of the right to exercise coercion, the regulation of military expeditions and the freedom of the public prosecutor from administrative control. . . .

The Free State was created, with the consent of the entire world, twenty years ago, by a single will which, as is well-known, allied to itself the services of Stanley in the object of opening central Africa to civilisation and which alone, without the aid of any one, bore the entire expense of its establishment. Its origin came from the acquiescence of the native chiefs and the personal efforts of its creator.

The Powers have recognised its sovereign existence, but without contributing either to the work in view or to its development, and naturally without any idea of assistance or of guardianship—a notion incompatible with the title *Independent* or *Free* which was given to the State.

For several years the young State lived solely upon the grants made by its founder. Then Belgium lent a generous aid, and now that its organisation has assumed considerable importance, it can rely upon its own resources.

This is, we think, an exceptional situation which differs essentially from that of the colonies, properly so called, in Africa or elsewhere, and one which should be kept in mind.

The State will be able to carry out progressively the reforms we propose. They will occasion an increase in expenditures; but it would fail in the discharge of its duty if, from the present moment, it did not employ every available means to realise the wishes formulated in this Report and which, we repeat, are inspired by the interests of the native population.

Please accept, Mr. Secretary of State, the assurance of our high consideration.

President of the Commission of Enquiry:

EDMOND JANSSENS.

Commissioners:

GIACOMO NISCO, E. DE SCHUMACHER.

Secretary: Translator:
  V. DENYN. HENRI GRÉGOIRE.

26

BELGIAN PARLIAMENT

Debates on the Congo Free State

February–March 1906

These Belgian parliamentary debates reflect the domestic political controversy over the report on the Congo Free State by the commission of inquiry (Document 25). In this selection, members of parliament discuss whether or not the Belgian government has a right to intervene in the Congo Free State. Émile Vandervelde (1866–1938), who opened the debates, was the most prominent Belgian critic of the Congo Free State. A member of parliament since 1894 and a socialist, he advanced a radical critique of the Congo Free State and imperialism that resembles the critiques by John Hobson and Edmund Morel (Documents 20 and 21), though these Britons were not socialists but radical liberals. Auguste Beernaert (1829–1912), who closed the debates, was prime minister of Belgium between 1884 and 1894, a difficult period in the development of the Congo Free State during which Leopold II secured crucial loans from the Belgian government. By 1906, when these debates took place,

Verbatim Report of the Five Days' Congo Debate in the Belgian House of Representatives, trans. E. D. Morel (Liverpool: John Richardson & Sons, 1906), 28–31, 37, 40, 46, 49–51, 75, 147–48.

*Beernaert conveyed disillusionment with the Congo Free State. Three
years later, in 1909, he would win the Nobel Peace Prize for his work at
the International Court of Arbitration at The Hague. As shown in the
extracts here, how do these members of parliament differ in their under-
standings of race and the role of religion in empire?*

M. VANDERVELDE:—The revenues of the *Domaine de la Couronne* [Crown
Domain] have been used in our country towards the resurrection of
a personal power, whose dominating and corrupting influence inter-
feres with the mechanism of our Parliamentary institutions (applause
on the Socialist benches). We shall be told, no doubt, that the money
of the *Domaine de la Couronne* is profitable to Belgium; that the King
has only in view the interests of Belgium; that the property which he
acquires will some day return to Belgium; I reply that, alongside the
presents which are given us, sacrifices are imposed upon us. Boast,
for instance, is made of the present of 5,000,000 francs, which served
to construct the triumphal arch, the moneys for which the House
refused to vote. We are told that, at the death of the King, other advantages will be granted us, and there is an attempt to forget that between
the Sovereign of the Congo State and the Belgian Government, all
that exists is a system of tit for tat.

I will pay your arch on condition that you give me the tunnel, costing
3,000,000 francs, which connects my Palace at Laeken with the main
railway line.

I will give you some millions at my death, on condition that you place
at my disposal, without interest, the 31,000,000 francs which Belgium
has advanced to the Congo State. I will give you later the *Domaine de la
Couronne*, on condition that the day upon which you annex the Congo
you will take over at the same time its Public Debt.

The result of all this is that, far from profiting, we are running the
risk of losing, and that, meantime, the Sovereign of the Congo, who
is also the King of the Belgians, escapes from Parliamentary control,
can execute such public works as may please him, can spread money
broadcast, and spend 30,000,000 francs on the improvement of his
Palace at Laeken, saying to himself that, as a last resort, it is Belgium
which will have to pay (applause on the Socialist benches).

It is essential, gentlemen, that we should see quite clearly, as far as
is possible, into the finances of the Congo State. I say as far as is possible, because, owing to the negligence of the Belgian Government,

we are very insufficiently informed. Formerly, in exchange for the loan of 31,000,000 francs, which Belgium made to the Congo State, Belgium had the right to claim information on the financial situation. On this head we received an account of the receipts and expenditure of the Congo State in 1890, 1891, 1892 and 1893. From that date, nothing! And in 1900, notwithstanding the opposition of men like Messieurs Beernaert and De Lantsheere, the Houses decided that the Congo State would no longer be called upon to furnish us with any information, and that its option to contract loans would be henceforth unlimited. What have been the results of this financial emancipation? M. Cattier has endeavoured to calculate them in his book. He has taken the interest on loans paid each year by the State, and by carefully worked-out calculations he has capitalised them. Here are the results of his calculations. The total amount of the debt was—

In	1898	. . .	2,283,000	francs.
„	1899	. . .	12,533,000	„
„	1900	. . .	12,783,000	„
„	1901	. . .	15,672,000	„
„	1902	. . .	41,973,000	„
„	1903	. . .	35,939,000	„
„	1904	. . .	55,939,000	„
„	1905	. . .	80,631,000	„

And to this figure of 80,000,000 francs must be added the 31,000,000 lent by Belgium, and the net product of the loan on the lottery system—net product which M. Cattier estimates at 50 millions, which makes, independently of the sum lent by Belgium, an approximate total of 130 millions, which represents the debt of the Congo State to-day, a debt which, in the case of annexation, will have to be taken over by Belgium.

M. BERTRAND:—Here is the danger!

M. VANDERVELDE:—Was I right in saying just now that the sumptuary works carried out at Laeken, in Brussels, or in Ostend, are being constructed with the money of the Belgian taxpayer? No doubt, gentlemen, I shall be told that the figures which I have indicated are merely estimates. I recognise it, but let us then be given specific figures. Let us be reassured as to the future. Let us have light upon a situation which ought to pre-occupy us, because, when all is said and done, we are incurring, all of us, a heavy responsibility in allowing, every day, a state of affairs to be aggravated, a state of affairs the consequences of which the Belgian people will ultimately be called upon to bear.

What is particularly deplorable in this state of affairs is, that it seems the 130 millions borrowed by the Congo State have not been utilised in the development of the Colony. Indeed, so far as any value can be attached to the financial estimates published each year by the Congo State, the total deficit of the Congo State has amounted to 27 million francs only. Now, 130 million francs have been borrowed. If we subtract the 27 million francs from the 130 million francs, there remain over 103 million francs, which seem to have been utilised and expended elsewhere than in the Congo. Gentlemen, metropolises have sometimes been known, may still be known, which exploit their Colonies, and make use of the profits derived therefrom to carry out public works elsewhere than in those Colonies. But the Congo State has alone given to the world this strange sight of a Colonial Government which borrows money on its Colony, in order to undertake speculative enterprises in other Continents and in other ways, for instance, in China and in Belgium! I shall not fail, no doubt, to be told, "You are alarmed at this Congo debt, but you forget the other side, namely the portfolio of the Congo State."

It is true, gentlemen, that the stock which this portfolio contains brings in about the same as, or a little less than, the interest on the public debt. But the majority of this stock consists of shares in Congolese Companies; there are the shares of the A.B.I.R., of the Anversoise Company, and similar companies. So long as the present system continues, all goes well. As long as the present frantic exploitation of ivory, copal, and rubber continues, all is well. But when the ivory, copal and rubber do not come forward in the same quantities, when the present system of oppression of the natives has disappeared, things will altogether change. Then will the era of deficits commence; then the portfolio will no longer be equivalent to the public debt, and we shall experience all the disadvantages of a state of affairs from which others will have reaped all the profits (applause on the extreme left). This, gentlemen, is the situation from a financial point of view, and I do not think there is any one amongst you who ought not to be perturbed thereby. The situation, I repeat, is all the graver since the temporary prosperity of the Congo State depends exclusively upon the system of oppression imposed upon the natives.

Now, gentlemen, this system must disappear; it is condemned to disappear. From the moment that its existence is known, it is doomed.

The only question which you have to consider to-day is the direction whence reform is to come. Will it come from the Congo State itself, or from the intervention of the Powers, or, finally, from Belgian initiative?

From the Congo State itself! In this respect I am profoundly convinced that the Congo State is powerless to reform itself. The example of Russia proves that absolutism cannot reform itself. It is reformed or it is ended. (Applause on the extreme left.)

I am all the more justified in thinking that this is so when even the Commissioners of Enquiry, to whose impartiality and good faith, I have referred merely propose insignificant measures, mere palliatives. They uphold the system of forced labour, and they adopt the thesis defended a few days ago only, by M. Rolin, in the Review of the University of Brussels, that coercion is indispensable in tropical regions, that forced labour is necessary, that slavery is legitimate. . . .

To M. Rolin, therefore, who professes to believe that forced labour is necessary, the Congress of Colonial Sociology, at which he, I think, assisted, replies unanimously that forced labour is not necessary. In his article in the aforesaid Review, Professor Rolin attacked me, because I said that, in defending this principle, laid down by the Congress of Colonial Sociology, I was a radical. The word "radical," in his mind, means a man who considers that slavery is always intolerable, that the taking of hostages is criminal, that punitive expeditions are atrocious, and that it is indispensable to stamp out all disguised forms of slavery. In this respect, it is true, I am a radical, and I am sure that my friend M. Lorand will subscribe to the same sentiments.

But I return to what I was saying just now, viz., the absolute impossibility of expecting serious reforms from the Congo State, and I find the proof of this in the composition, which is at least strange, of the Commission of Reforms established after the enquiry. This Commission is composed of fourteen members. Amongst them there are four before whose independence I bow once more. These four are Messieurs Van Maldeghem, Janssens, Nys[1] and Davignon.

On the other hand, there are seven who are officials of the Congo State, that is to say, of the principal accused party, namely, Messieurs de Cuvelier, Droogmaus, Capt. Tombeur, Capt. Chenot, Gohr, Arnold, and Capt. Liebrechts, who certainly has incurred the largest part of

[1]Maitre Nys is a jurist, who has consistently defended, on juridical grounds, the claims applied by King Leopold to the land, the produce of the soil, and the labour of the Congo people, which claims constitute the bed-rock of the Congo system, and the enforcement of which claims is the explanation of the abominations without which that system is incapable of being maintained. See, further on, M. Lorand's comments upon these juridical white-washings. [All footnotes from original document.]

responsibility in the organisation of the system of exploitation of the natives. I find also on this Commission Colonel Fivé, who was the agent of the King in Persia and China, and M. de Hemptinne, of the Kassai[2] Society, and finally, what is almost unimaginable, M. Mols,[3] Administrator of the A.B.I.R., that is to say, of the Company against whom the frightful crimes related in the Report of the Commission are brought!

It is precisely as though one called in a slave-trader to a conference to abolish the slave trade! Under these conditions, how is it possible to hope that this Commission will bring about serious reforms? I notice that none of the men who have done good work on the Congo form part of it, and I do not find the name of Dhanis, nor do I find the names of Wangermee, Lemaire or Cambier. Neither do I see a solitary representative of the Catholic Missions. . . .

M. DE FAVEREAU:—By what right could we intervene in the internal affairs of the Congo State? M. Vandervelde cited Article 6 of the General Act of Berlin, but this Article is drawn up in the vaguest terms. Where, in the Act of the Conference of Berlin, does the honourable member see that the signatory Powers have the right, reciprocally, of controlling the fulfilment of the obligations contained in that article? If the honourable member knew the protocols of that Act, he would be aware that, on the contrary, the endeavour of the plenipotentiaries assembled at Berlin was to respect the sovereignty of the Powers having possessions in the Congo Basin. It would be contrary to all principles of international law that a Government should interfere with the internal administration of a Sovereign State. . . .

M. DE FAVEREAU:—Would it not have been wiser and more equitable to have waited until the Commission of Reforms had accomplished its labours before pronouncing its condemnation? The speech of the honourable member overlooks a fact, which appears to me to overshadow the whole situation. It is not possible to remove a population from the frightful barbarism in which it has grovelled for so many centuries, whose morality is often low and degraded, without compelling it to make a considerable effort to which its characteristics and its inveterate habits are opposed.

M. A. DAENS:—The means chosen is extermination.

M. LORAND:—Quite so.

---

[2]In which the Congo Government holds fifty per cent of the shares, and whose administration it controls.

[3]M. Mols is on intimate terms with King Leopold. He it is who is interested in and practically controls a number of the so-called "French" Concessionnaire Companies, whose exploits in the French Congo have brought that French Dependency to its present pass.

M. DE FAVEREAU:—Absurd!

M. LORAND:—The results of the Commission's inquiry prove it. The population is exploited to such a degree, by such methods, that depopulation is rapid; that is what the impartial men who composed the Commission have recognised.

M. DE FAVEREAU:—M. Vandervelde suggests to the Belgian Government various means of action in regard to the Congo State. I have given the reasons which are opposed to our intervention, reasons of law and of fact. . . .

M. DE FAVEREAU:—I regret that, in the heart of the Belgian Parliament, a work like the Congo enterprise, which redounds to the honour of those who have devoted themselves to it body and soul, should be attacked by the leader of one of the Parliamentary Parties, who is thus furnishing weapons to those who are conducting an abominable Press campaign against this grand work.

M. VANDERVELDE:—It is the Commission of Inquiry which furnishes those weapons, not I.

M. DE FAVEREAU:—I am glad that the House has resolved to distribute the Report to each of its members. I ask them to read it with calmness and impartiality, and to purge their judgment of all passion.

M. VANDERVELDE:—It is not necessary to comment [on] it.

M. DE FAVEREAU:—And to take note of it without partiality.

M. ROGER:—The partiality lies with you.

M. DE FAVEREAU:—This grand work is above your attacks.

M. LEONARD:—This is absurd. All that you are saying is foreign to the debate.

M. DE FAVEREAU:—It is above contemptible attacks, both by the spirit which has inspired it and by the thought which has dictated the improvements and the reforms to be incorporated in it.

M. VANDERVELDE:—It is not above the duties of humanity.

M. DE FAVEREAU:—Thanks to the labours of the Commission of Inquiry, thanks to the labours of the Commission of Reforms, it will be possible to give to our future Colony an Administration which will bear comparison with that of the best administered Colonies. . . .

Speech by M. Verhaegen

M. VERHAEGEN:— . . . Catholic missionaries, nearly all Belgians, hastened to comply with the appeal of the Congo State, which answered at the same time to the suggestions of their own hearts, and proceeded to Central Africa. They settled in the spots assigned to them without any thought of the dangers of the climate. Young and old rivalled one another in ardour, hard for themselves, tender for the unhappy natives, a splendid band, before whom I bow with respect, recruited from all social classes, and amongst whom I note the son of our sympathetic colleague, M. Van Naeman; the missionaries have laboured incessantly on the Congo; much money has been spent by them, through the charity of Belgian Catholics. They have sacrificed their health; many have died, or have only returned to die.

What did they go out there for? To collect ivory, rubber, or gold? Better than that. To receive substantial salaries? To receive honours, or a name on the scroll of history? Better still. They have received, and they receive every day, the blessings of the natives. They bring the word and the love of God to the land of Africa. They are expanding Christian civilisation in the Congo—that is to say, the civilisation which has made Europe. Thanks to the missionaries, thanks to the King, who opened the road for them, and who appealed to them, deserving, therefore, the gratitude of all civilised humanity, millions of negroes, plunged in an abyss of degradation, have seen the light which the Saviour brought into the world. They have heard, and they have had practised towards them, the law which dominates, and which at the same time summarises, all divine teaching, "Love one another." Thanks to the missionaries, native customs in the regions which they evangelise have become purer. The secular humiliation in which woman is placed has been altered for a higher ideal, family life has taken hold in the Congo. Monogamy has become respected. The native begins to understand that from the law of work a higher social standard emanates. Christianity will put an end to the material and moral degradation of populations plunged for many centuries in the backwash of barbarism. . . .

What figures cannot show, is the admiration which is inspired in the native by the apostolic life of these religious men, the veneration and the confidence with which the latter are surrounded, the prodigious influence exercised upon the natives by the absolute unselfishness of which the missionaries give an example. Such, gentlemen, is the secret of their power. They are expanding the field of civilisation, without coercion, solely by their moral ascendancy, and one can say that they alone really civilise the native, because too often certain servants of the State, and certain agents of the Companies propagate around them nothing but terror and hatred. . . .

M. WOESTE:—Alongside this primary error there is a secondary one, and that is the idea that a barbarous country can be governed on the lines of a civilised country. No doubt we must approximate to these lines as much as possible, but account must be taken of the mental condition of those whose civilisation is aimed at. Proceedings which might have full success in our country, would be doomed there to complete sterility. Where you have an advanced state of civilisation, force must be set aside as much as possible. In barbarous countries, among infant peoples, coercion is often necessary; authority must be felt, in order to be respected. It is due to the influence of the two errors which I am pointing out that so many inaccurate judgments have been pronounced, and are still pronounced, on the Congo State. The Congo State is looked upon, and I understand the desire up to a certain point, as another Belgium. I hope, gentlemen, it may be so one day; but, before this day comes, we must admit the necessity in which the governing element finds itself of often employing means other than those which are current in our civilised Europe. The Belgian Government is asked what it means to do to prevent the state of affairs which has been pointed out, as if the Belgian Government were the Government of the Congo State! When one goes to the root of matters, it will be recognised that the personality aimed at here is the Sovereign of the Congo State himself. . . .

M. BEERNAERT:— . . . Well, gentlemen, when in the opening words of my Resolution, I ask you to applaud once more the grandeur of the conception, the liberal and generous spirit with which the Congo was admitted into the family of nations, the numberless sacrifices of all kinds which have been made for it, even of life itself, am I not entitled to rely upon your universal approval? (General assent.)

But, in the course of the last few years, grave divergencies have arisen in the vast basin of Central Africa, notably as regards the organisation of property, of labour, and of taxation, and on this subject fierce polemics have taken place in Belgium and elsewhere. . . . It is true that we have seen some of our writers declare that the negro is barely a man, and that the negress is only cattle! (Outcry.)

M. JANSON:—These views have no echo in the country (applause on the opposition benches). These ideas contain their own refutation, and do not redound to the honour of those who put them forward (applause on the same benches).

M. BEERNAERT:—I am not astonished to hear M. Janson express in this matter an opinion similar to mine. Yes, certainly these sentiments find no echo in our country, but in reading them one is conscious of the most painful and the most detestable impression (applause on the same benches). One asks one's self how it can be possible that, after nineteen centuries of Christianity, arguments can be revived which thinkers already found intolerable before Christianity appeared in the world (loud applause).

M. DE SMET DE NAEYER:—These arguments have never found defenders in Parliament.

M. BEERNAERT:—I am convinced of it, and it was good to make it plain. Apart from those questions of principle, grave abuses have been committed, and not only in the Congo, nor even in Africa only, but nearly everywhere where colonies exist.

27

THE REVEREND JOHN HARRIS

Letter to W. T. Lamont, His Britannic Majesty's Consul at Boma

January 16, 1912

John Harris (1874–1940) and his wife, Alice (1870–1970), were members of the Congo Balolo Mission, stationed at Baringa, in the territory of the Anglo-Belgian India Rubber and Exploration Company (ABIR) between 1898 and 1905. They played leading roles in the Congo reform campaign in Britain through both eyewitness testimony and their organizational skills. They conducted and managed thousands of lantern slide lectures for the general public and established a network of local auxiliaries across Britain. As the Congo reform campaign began to dissipate, the Harrises became joint secretaries of the recently amalgamated British and Foreign Anti-Slavery and Aborigines' Protection Society in 1909.[1] With authorization from the Belgian government, they returned to Congo in 1911 and conducted an investigative tour for several months. In this letter to the British consul at Boma, John Harris observes positive changes in Congo since its annexation by Belgium in 1908, but he also issues warnings regarding ongoing labor exploitation and violations of Africans' property

---

[1]This organization was a combination of the British and Foreign Anti-Slavery Society and the Aborigines' Protection Society.

E. D. Morel Collection, Archives of the London School of Economics, F8/file 78.

rights. How do the Harrises' backgrounds and the audience for which John Harris wrote this report influence your understanding of its significance? In view of this final document, and looking back on other documents by critics of the Congo Free State in this collection, would you generally characterize humanitarians at the turn of the twentieth century as opponents or supporters of the civilizing mission? Is this historical humanitarianism fundamentally similar to or different from contemporary humanitarianism?

To His Britannic Majesty's Consul.

Sir:

I am glad to respond to your suggestion that I should record in writing very briefly and in general terms the main points upon which our conversations have turned.

My wife and I have been marching, canoeing, and travelling by steamers through the Upper Congo regions for between seven and eight months, and have covered in our journeys something like 5,000 miles of territory, most of which has been hinterland travel and a great deal of this in circumstances of real difficulty and not a little danger. . . .

The necessary brevity of this letter permits of my mentioning only the leading features of the existing situation on the Congo.

The first is the disappearance of systematic brutality; atrocities and acts of a barbarous nature may occur from time to time in the more isolated parts, but the general trend of opinion and activity is now firmly set against them. This new condition of affairs is undoubtedly due in a large measure to the reform of M. [Jules] Renkin [the Colonial Minister], but still more I think to the well known attitude of the present occupant of the Belgian throne [Albert I, nephew of Leopold II].

I must confess, however, to greater anxiety with regard to the future, and there are several features which appear to me to present even grave possibilities. . . .

There is a tendency to regard all undertakings by the Government as works of public utility, and, as such, justifying forced labour. Roads, bridges, and creek-clearing, legitimately come under a category of works of general benefit, but these are quite different from the profit-bearing enterprises of telegraphs, railways, riverine transport, and even plantations of rubber and cocoa.

M. Renkin's advertised programme includes the laying down of 50,000 acres of rubber, which will mean something over 20 million trees, and these, with the existing 10 to 15 millions, will require from 50,000 to

80,000 labourers. The contract labour on these plantations is today very largely impressed labour, or as the Director of one Commercial Company humourously termed it "volunteers by the rope," i.e., recruited, and then sent to the plantations roped neck to neck.

The securing of this labour will be facilitated by the Chefferie [chiefdom] system [a system of indirect rule through government-appointed Congolese chiefs], which is becoming very much like the old sentry system under King Leopold's Administration. Almost every charge made against the sentries, with the exception of murder, may be sustained against the Chefferies as a whole, nor is this surprising when it is realized that many of the old criminal sentries have actually been promoted to the position of Chefferie.

Closely allied to the foregoing is the absence of land legislation for the natives, and this again is a root cause of maladministration. The old Congo State refused to recognize the ordinary communal tenure of the natives. Not only so, King Leopold substituted nothing for it, and the Belgian Government maintains a like position with the result that the economic expansion of the native is immobilised, and they must buy land from Brussels if they desire to make plantations beyond the village boundary. This situation is surely grotesque where millions of acres of land are lying idle. The object appears to be that of restricting the native to the position of a labourer.

I emphasize, therefore, these three points,—all interwoven—state commerce, forced contract labour, and the absence of equitable land legislation. I repeat that the abolition of the first would carry with it the disappearance of forced labour, and provide reasonable security in land tenure for the natives.

I shall hope to have an early opportunity upon our return of urging upon [Foreign Secretary] Sir Edward Grey the importance of securing the most explicit guarantees upon these three features precedent to British recognition of the transfer. Also with reference to our responsibilities under the Conventions and Acts by which the Congo has become a Belgian Colony. The latter point may seem irrelevant, or at least superfluous, but in view of the attitude of many Belgians out here, coupled with certain language used in Brussels to British Ministers, it has become a matter of considerable moment.

The prevailing desire for British recognition appears to be based upon the strange notion that once this takes place our responsibilities under those instruments cease to exist.

Other points of subsidiary importance are the continued employment of old Congo State officials; the paucity of judicial officers, particularly of the higher ranks; no alternative for a tax in coin; the lack of benefits in return for taxation; the almost farcical constitution of the Congo Aborigines Protection Committee; and the general lack of effective administration, particularly in the toleration of widespread native slavery.

I have written with extreme brevity, partly through lack of time, but also because I know you merely wish for a short statement, but this has necessarily precluded the mention of points, important in themselves, but which are more or less involved in the larger issues.

I trust you will feel free to use this letter in any way short of publication; possibly Sir Francis Hyde Villiers [Minister to Belgium] and Sir Arthur Hardinge [the previous Minister to Belgium, 1906–1911] (both of whom I have the pleasure of knowing) would like to have a copy.

I am,
Yours faithfully,
(Signed) JOHN H. HARRIS.

A Chronology of Congo and the
Congo Free State
(1860–1914)

1860s Slave traders backed by the sultan of Zanzibar invade the eastern Congo.

1865 Leopold II becomes king of Belgium.

1876 *September* Leopold hosts the Brussels Geographical Conference. The conference creates the International African Association for the Exploration and Civilization of Central Africa and elects Leopold as the association's president.

1877 *August 9* Henry Stanley arrives at the mouth of the Congo River, having tracked its course in 999 days.

1878 *November* Leopold and international investors found the Committee for Studies of the Upper Congo.

1879 *August 15* Stanley returns to the Congo River to work on behalf of the Committee for Studies of the Upper Congo.

        December Committee for Studies of the Upper Congo renamed International Association of the Congo (IAC).

**Early
1880s** First epidemics of smallpox spread through Congo's central basin.

1881 *December 3* Stanley launches the first steamboat at Stanley Pool (now Malebo Pool) for the exploration and conquest of the upper river on behalf of the IAC.

1883 Stanley establishes the easternmost station of the IAC at Stanley Falls (now Boyoma Falls).

**1884–
1885** *November 15, 1884–February 23, 1885* Berlin Conference convenes under the auspices of the German chancellor, Otto von Bismarck; delegates sign the Berlin Act.

1885 *August 1* Leopold announces the founding of the Congo Free State.

1886–
1888   Congo Free State organizes the *force publique*, a military composed of African soldiers and European officers.

1887   *August*   Tippu Tip becomes governor of the Stanley Falls District.

1889   John Dunlop begins the mass manufacture of pneumatic tires for bicycles.

1889–
1890   *November 18, 1889–July 2, 1890*   Brussels Conference convenes under the auspices of Leopold and Cardinal Lavigerie to coordinate European policies against slave trading and liquor and arms trafficking in Africa; delegates sign the Brussels Conference Act.

1890
or
1891   Tippu Tip leaves his post as governor.

1890   Congo Free State begins construction of the Matadi-Léopoldville railway to circumvent the Congo River's cataracts and facilitate access to the upper river above Malebo Pool.

1891   Katanga Company founded.

             Congo Free State institutes a new system of local administration based on the appointment of chiefs as agents of the state.

             December 12   Leopold secretly signs a decree arrogating all "vacant lands" within the Congo Free State. This decree forms the legal basis of the vast territory known as the *Domaine Privé*.

             December 20   Soldiers of the Congo Free State assert the state's rule over the Katanga region.

1892   *August*   Anglo-Belgian India Rubber and Exploration Company (ABIR), Company of Antwerp for Trade in Congo, and Anonymous Belgian Company for Trade in Upper-Congo founded to exploit the rain forests in the region of the Lopori and Maringa rivers.

1892–
1894   Congo Free State wages a major military campaign against Zanzibari slave traders in eastern Congo.

1896   Rubber replaces ivory as the Congo Free State's main export to Europe.

1897   *February*   Mutiny by the *force publique* at Ndirfi.

1898   *March*   Congo Free State completes construction of the Matadi-Léopoldville railway.

1901   Peak rubber production in the Congo Free State.

December   Leopold grants a monopoly to the Kasai Company over trade in rubber, ivory, and other commodities in the Kasai region.

1904   *February*   Roger Casement's consular report on the Congo Free State published by the British Parliament.

March 23   Congo Reform Association founded in Liverpool, England.

1905   *October 31*   Congo Free State's Commission of Enquiry publishes report on the administration and conditions of Congo.

1906   *February–March*   Belgian parliament engages in five days of debate on the Congo Free State.

September 12   Both ABIR and the Company of Antwerp turn over the administration of their concessions to the Congo Free State.

1908   *November 15*   Belgian government annexes the Congo Free State after prolonged negotiations with Leopold.

1909   *December 17*   Leopold II dies. He is succeeded as king by his nephew, Albert.

1909– 1912   Belgian government of Congo fixes the annual rate of taxation for Congolese subjects, divests itself from European commercial firms, extends its administration and judicial systems to the upper river, and reforms the territorial structure of its administrative districts.

1913   *June 16*   Congo Reform Association holds its final meeting in London.

1914   *August 3*   Germany invades Belgium to outflank French forces at the outset of the First World War.

August 4   As an ally of Belgium, Great Britain declares war on Germany.

Questions for Consideration

1. How do the Congolese and European sources in this volume vary in their assessments of how the lives of Congolese peoples changed under the Congo Free State?

2. How do the Congolese and European critics of the Congo Free State vary in describing the causes of the crisis in Congo and the possible solutions to this crisis?

3. According to the Congolese sources, what were the strengths and weaknesses of the Congo Free State?

4. According to Congolese and European sources, when and how was the brutality of the Congo Free State mitigated?

5. How are the principles advocated by David Livingstone (Document 1) similar to those advocated by King Leopold II (Document 2) and European leaders at the Berlin Conference (Document 5)? How are they different?

6. How are the principles articulated in the Berlin Act (Document 5) similar to those advocated by Edmund Morel and the Congo Reform Association (Document 21)? How are they different?

7. What were the main motives of those who condemned the Congo Free State and called for reforms in the European press?

8. Compare and contrast the racial ideas of the defenders and critics of the Congo Free State.

9. What were the criticisms that Belgians leveled at Leopold II and the Congo Free State?

10. In what ways was the Congo Free State a product of European industrialization?

11. What are the strengths and limitations of the sources supportive of the Congo Free State and those critical of the Congo Free State as historical evidence?

12. What are the strengths and limitations of atrocity photographs (Document 23) and cartoons (Document 24) as historical evidence?

Selected Bibliography

GENERAL

Birmingham, David, and Phyllis Martin, eds. *History of Central Africa*. Vol. 2. New York: Longman, 1983.

Boahen, A. Adu, ed. *General History of Africa: Africa under Colonial Domination, 1880–1935*. London: UNESCO, 1985.

Conklin, Alice. "Colonialism and Human Rights: A Contradiction in Terms? The Case of France and West Africa, 1895–1914." *American Historical Review* 103, no. 2 (April 1998): 419–42.

Cooper, Frederick. "Conditions Analogous to Slavery: Imperialism and Free Labor Ideology in Africa." In *Beyond Slavery*, edited by Frederick Cooper, Thomas C. Holt, and Rebecca J. Scott, 107–56. Chapel Hill: University of North Carolina Press, 2000.

Daughton, J. P. *An Empire Divided: Religion, Republicanism, and the Making of French Colonialism, 1880–1914*. Oxford: Oxford University Press, 2006.

Fieldhouse, D. K. *Economics and Empire, 1830–1914*. Ithaca. N.Y.: Cornell University Press, 1973.

Förster, Stig, Wolfgang Mommsen, and Ronald Robinson, eds. *Bismarck, Europe and Africa: The Berlin Africa Conference, 1884–1885*. Oxford: Oxford University Press, 1988.

Gifford, Prosser, and Wm. Roger Louis, eds. *Britain and Germany in Africa: Imperial Rivalry and Colonial Rule*. New Haven, Conn.: Yale University Press, 1967.

Gordon, David M. *Invisible Agents: Spirits in a Central African History*. Athens: Ohio University Press, 2012.

Hochschild, Adam. *King Leopold's Ghost*. Boston: Houghton Mifflin, 1999.

Jeal, Tim. *Stanley: The Impossible Life of Africa's Greatest Explorer*. New Haven, Conn.: Yale University Press, 2007.

Oliver, Roland, and G. N. Sanderson, eds. *The Cambridge History of Africa*. Vol. 6, *1870–1905*. Cambridge: Cambridge University Press, 1985.

Robinson, Ronald, and John Gallagher, with Alice Denny. *Africa and the Victorians: The Climax of Imperialism in the Dark Continent*. New York: St. Martin's Press, 1961.

Vansina, Jan. *Paths in the Rainforests: Toward a History of Political Tradition in Equatorial Africa*. Madison: University of Wisconsin Press, 1990.

THE CONGOLESE PEOPLES

De Craemer, Willy, Jan Vansina, and Renee C. Fox. "Religious Movements in Central Africa: A Theoretical Study." *Comparative Studies in Society and History* 18, no. 4 (October 1976): 458–75.

Fabian, Johannes. *Language and Colonial Power: The Appropriation of Swahili in the Former Belgian Congo, 1880–1938*. Berkeley: University of California Press, 1991.

Harms, Robert. *River of Wealth, River of Sorrow: The Central Zaire Basin in the Era of the Slave and Ivory Trade, 1500–1891*. New Haven, Conn.: Yale University Press, 1981.

Hunt, Nancy Rose. *A Colonial Lexicon: Of Birth Ritual, Medicalization, and Mobility in the Congo*. Durham, N.C.: Duke University Press, 1999.

Likaka, Osumaka. *Naming Colonialism: History and Collective Memory in the Congo, 1870–1960*. Madison: University of Wisconsin Press, 2009.

MacGaffey, Wyatt. "Economic and Social Dimensions of Kongo Slavery." In *Slavery in Africa: Historical and Anthropological Perspectives*, edited by Suzanne Miers and Igor Kopytoff, 235–57. Madison: University of Wisconsin Press, 1977.

———. *Kongo Political Culture: The Conceptual Challenge of the Particular*. Bloomington: Indiana University Press, 2000.

Nelson, Samuel H. *Colonialism in the Congo Basin, 1880–1940*. Athens: Ohio University Center for International Studies, 1994.

Northrup, David. *Beyond the Bend in the River: African Labor in Eastern Zaire, 1865–1940*. Athens: Ohio University Center for International Studies, 1988.

Van Reybrouck, David. *Congo: The Epic History of a People*. New York: Ecco, 2010.

Vansina, Jan. *Being Colonized: The Kuba Experience in Rural Congo, 1880–1960*. Madison: University of Wisconsin Press, 2010.

———. *Kingdoms of the Savanna: A History of Central African States until European Occupation*. Madison: University of Wisconsin Press, 1967.

———. *The Tio Kingdom of the Middle Congo, 1880–1892*. London: Oxford University Press for the International African Institute, 1973.

BELGIUM, THE CONGO FREE STATE, AND CONCESSIONAIRE COMPANIES

Gann, L. H., and Peter Duignan. *The Rulers of Belgian Africa, 1884–1914*. Princeton, N.J.: Princeton University Press, 1979.

Harms, Robert. "King Leopold's Bonds." In *The Origins of Value*, edited by William Goetzmann and K. Geert Rouwenhorst, 343–57. Oxford: Oxford University Press, 2005.

————. "The World ABIR Made: The Maringa-Lopori Basin, 1885–1903." *African Economic History* 22 (1983): 125–39.

Hunt, Nancy Rose. *A Nervous State: Violence, Remedies, and Reverie in Colonial Congo*. Durham, N.C.: Duke University Press, 2016.

Laqua, Daniel. *The Age of Internationalism and Belgium, 1880–1930: Peace, Progress and Prestige*. Manchester, U.K.: Manchester University Press, 2013.

Roes, Aldwin. "Towards a History of Mass Violence in the État Indépendant du Congo, 1885–1908." *South African Historical Journal* 62, no. 4 (2010): 634–70.

Stengers, Jean. "King Leopold's Congo, 1886–1908." In *The Cambridge History of Africa*, vol. 6, *1870–1905*, edited by Roland Oliver and G. N. Sanderson, 315–57. Cambridge: Cambridge University Press, 1985.

Vanthemsche, Guy. *Belgium and the Congo, 1885–1980*. Cambridge: Cambridge University Press, 2012.

MISSIONARIES

Benedetto, Robert, ed. *Presbyterian Reformers in Central Africa: A Documentary Account of the American Presbyterian Congo Mission and the Human Rights Struggle in the Congo, 1890–1918*. Leiden: E. J. Brill, 1996.

Grant, Kevin. "Christian Critics of Empire: Missionaries, Lantern Lectures, and the Congo Reform Campaign in Britain." In *The Rise and Fall of Modern Empires*, vol. 4, *Reactions to Colonialism*, edited by Martin Shipway, 91–122. London: Ashgate, 2013.

Lagergren, David. *Mission and State in the Congo, 1885–1903*. Lund, Sweden: Gleerup, 1970.

THE CONGO CONTROVERSY AND HUMANITARIANISM

Drescher, Seymour. *Abolition: A History of Slavery and Antislavery*. Cambridge: Cambridge University Press, 2009, especially chap. 13, "Emancipation in the Old World, 1880s–1920s."

Grant, Kevin, "The Limits of Exposure: Atrocity Photographs in the Congo Reform Campaign." In *Humanitarian Photography: A History*, edited by Heide Fehrenbach and Davide Rodogno, 64–88. Cambridge: Cambridge University Press, 2015.

————. *A Civilised Savagery: Britain and the New Slaveries in Africa, 1884–1926*. New York: Routledge, 2005.

Hunt, Nancy Rose. "An Acoustic Register, Tenacious Images, and Congolese Scenes of Rape and Repetition." *Cultural Anthropology* 23, no. 2 (2008): 220–53.

Laqua, Daniel. "The Tensions of Internationalism: Transnational Anti-Slavery in the 1880s and 1890s." *International History Review* 33, no. 4 (2011): 705–26.

Miers, Suzanne. *Britain and the Ending of the Slave Trade*. London: Longman, 1975.

Morel, E. D. *History of the Congo Reform Movement*. Edited by Wm. Roger Louis and Jean Stengers. Oxford: Clarendon Press, 1968.

Osborne, John B. "Wilfred G. Thesiger, Sir Edward Grey, and the British Campaign to Reform the Congo, 1905–9." *Journal of Imperial and Commonwealth History* 27, no. 1 (January 1999): 59–80.

Ó Síocháin, Séamus, and Michael O'Sullivan, eds. *The Eyes of Another Race: Roger Casement's Congo Report and 1903 Diary*. Dublin: University College Dublin Press, 2003.

Pavlakis, Dean. *British Humanitarianism and the Congo Reform Movement, 1896–1913*. Farnham, U.K.: Ashgate, 2015.

Twomey, Christina. "Framing Atrocity: Photography and Humanitarianism." *History of Photography* 36, no. 3 (2012): 255–64.

Index

abolition of slavery, 10–11, 32, 114
Abolition of Slavery Act of 1833, 47
Aborigines' Protection Society, 74
"Account of the Destruction of the Congo
Free State's Station at Stanley Falls in
an Attack by Zanzibari Slave Traders"
(Deane), 41–43
Affairs of West Africa, From" (Morel),
94–98
Afolembe, Nicolas, "Oral History regarding
Conditions in the Equateur District,"
66–70
Africa. *See also specific countries*
early European control of, 11–12
European expansion into, 9–11
explorers of, 39
internal slave trade, 5, 23, 31–32
Anglo-Belgian India Rubber and Exploration
Company (ABIR)
conditions under, 17, 59–74, 103–5, 117,
119, 133–36
founding of, 60n5, 138
land acquisition of, 13
legal authority of, 105–6, 119–20
profits from rubber boom, 15, 99
state ownership of, 16
Anglo-French entente of 1904, 11
Angola, 30–31
Anonymous Belgian Company for Trade in
Upper-Congo, 13, 59, 60n5, 138
Anti-Slavery Society. *See* British and Foreign
Anti-Slavery Society
atrocity photographs, 21–22, 108, 109f

Bakela people, 63, 65
Bangala people, 42–43, 96
Banks, Charles, 58–59, 58nn13–14, 75,
79–80
bartering
for ivory, 61–62
for land, 57, 57n3
for rubber, 61–62, 64, 70, 99
Batetlas people, 96
Beernaert, Auguste, 124–25, 132–33
Belgium
annexation of Congo, 22–23, 139
control of Congo, 11–18, 94–98
empire-building of, 9–11

German invasion of, 139
investigation of alleged abuses in Congo
Free State, 112–24
parliamentary debates on Congo Free
State, 124–33
Berlin Act of 1885
Articles V, VI, IX, and XIII reprinted,
38–40
Congo Free State governance and, 17,
21
pledge to care for Congolese people in,
11
signing of, 137
sovereignty of states and, 129
trade restrictions, 12–13
Bismarck, Otto von, 11
Bobangi people, 4
Boelaert, Edmond, 55, 59, 63, 66
Boongo, Antoine, "Oral History regarding
the Arrival of European Officers and
Missionaries at Wangata in the Equateur District," 55–59
Boyoma Falls (Stanley Falls), 10, 12, 41–43,
137–38
breech-loading rifles, 6
British and Foreign Anti-Slavery Society,
47–51
Brussels Conference of 1889–1890, 9, 12,
33, 138
Burrows, Guy, 13–14

Cameron, Verney Lovett, 9, 32, 48–49
cannibalism
civilizing mission and, 114
Congo Free State's condemnation of,
83–85
interior African peoples and, 37
of native army recruits, 96
prosecution for, 22
slave trade and, 100–101
Casement, Roger, 20–21
"Consular Report on the Congo Free
State to the British Foreign Secretary,"
98–108, 138
Casman, Guillaume "Katamandala," 56,
56n4
cassava root, 5
Catholic missionaries, 5, 12, 18, 77, 130–31

145